Time to
Write
Persuasively

A Five-Step Guide For Ambitious Researchers

Karyn Gonano

First published in 2023 by Karyn Gonano

© Karyn Gonano 2023
The moral rights of the author have been asserted

All inquiries should be made to the author.

A catalogue entry for this book is available from the National Library of Australia.

ISBN: 978-1-923007-28-4

Printed in Australia by McPherson's Printing
Book production and text design by Publish Central
Cover design by Pipeline Design

The paper this book is printed on is certified as environmentally friendly.

Contents

Introduction

If you're a researcher, you want your discoveries to have as much impact as possible on the world to make life easier, richer or safer for others. But exceptional researchers with brilliant ideas often lose grant applications. It's awful – the heartbreak and the frustration, sometimes after years of work. And many exceptional researchers with brilliant ideas win hundreds of thousands of dollars, get international speaking gigs and book deals, and their work changes the world. What is the difference between them? Their scientific knowledge? No. Their research topics? No. Their connections? No.

The latter are persuasive writers.

Are you certain of the positive impact your work could have on the planet? How is it then that you don't win grants, secure promotions or have your articles published? Yes, you can write well for your academic audience, but for your work to reach the wider world you need to learn to write for editors, grant committees and human resources departments. You must become more aware of the power your writing has to change the world. Perhaps you wish it was just about your work – but it's not.

It's beautiful to be a writer. Writing well enables you to express your thoughts so others can discover them and delight in them. This book will show you how to write persuasively, so you can reach – and influence – a much larger audience.

Universities have always been competitive places, and research facilities are always under financial pressure. It's not getting any better – if anything, it's getting tougher. To get that grant, stay on as a researcher or win the promotion, you have to have an impact with your research. At the same time, the world is overflowing with information and you have to stand out to achieve what you are trying to do.

Researchers are experts who want to solve problems, but writing about your research takes effort, deliberate intention and action. Writing articles, grant proposals, promotion documents and theses can feel challenging. You probably feel you never have enough time. And a prestigious title or position is no guarantee of success or good writing. You could be an emerging professor, associate professor or lecturer, or have a designer or lawyer title, but these will not help you if you can't write persuasively.

WHO AM I?

My passion for communication was born from standing in the United Nations headquarters in New York at the age of 18, seeing the world in one room. I thought if the world – shrunk into that one room – can communicate so effectively, then why not expand that principle so everyone communicates and works together? Today, I help university researchers and people in councils and commercial workplaces to write well and to make an impact. I've worked in Italy, helping businesspeople persuade the world about the value of their wine or fashion; helped IT gurus share that their tech expertise is at the forefront of computer science; and assisted professors who are doctors in universities to write about their pulmonary expertise and the toxicity of fungi. I've helped academics in Australia and Germany achieve promotions and win grants. I've helped with countless articles that were not only published but also highly praised. I've helped hundreds of thousands of dollars roll into researchers' bank accounts.

I've noticed women researchers can struggle and become marginalised. They are less practised at being confident putting their skills on display and claiming their expertise. And I've worked with men who struggle with the written word and promoting their research to make more impact. I've helped those of you with English as a second or third language turn your messages into succinct nuggets. And I've coached Australian corporations to communicate effectively and efficiently on large multinational projects in countries where English was not the primary language and the culture is different.

One of my clients, a local government organisation, won a bid to be recognised by UNESCO as a 'biosphere' and international site of excellence. And I've worked with TEDx speakers, getting their unique ideas out there and winning.

ABOUT THIS BOOK

I know you are a researcher first and a writer second. Or, you might not even think of yourself as a writer – but you must change that. The degree to which you change that view is the degree to which you will have a greater impact on the world. I'm putting decades of experience and knowledge of what you need into this book because I want everyone to hear your message.

While many of the tips and strategies I provide here would be useful to any writer of any non-fiction material, I have targeted the group I know needs this desperately. This book contains my fabulous five-step process that will help you write better than you ever imagined.

I've been working in universities for over 20 years, helping academics and researchers write grant applications and publications for journals. The biggest single problem I see is they never allow enough time to write. They rush. And in doing so, they undermine their own ability to impact the world. After reading this book you will not have to rush your writing anymore.

Irish playwright Oscar Wilde said, 'If you cannot write well, you cannot think well. If you cannot think well, others will do your thinking for you.' This is very true. In early 2010, a young up-and-coming researcher came into my office at the Queensland University of Technology, flustered. She asked me to check her document quickly, to make sure she got her funding application in on time. When I did, my heart sank. It was full of jargon, and difficult to understand. The critical ideas about her research's importance and why it mattered were missing. I had to tell her it would need a good bit of work. Her eyes filled with tears, and she said, 'I don't have time'. I replied, 'Even if you miss this round, the work we will do together will ensure you nail every funding round after that'. We applied techniques I will show you in this book. She didn't win that funding round, but she did get promoted and won funding soon after.

The book is in two parts. The first establishes why writing persuasively matters to you, why your research matters, why your researcher identity matters, and why writing to achieve impact matters. The second part is a detailed journey into the five steps of writing, demystifying the process and making you irresistible in the competitive world of research. We are going to look at the complexity of the problems you are facing. You'll be amazed at what I'm going to tell you and the difference it will make to your work.

Throughout the book you will find real-life examples that you can learn from, and activities that will get you started on the journey. And for ease of use the activities are all included again at the end of each chapter. You can go to my website klgcommunications.com.au for the full set of activities available in my Write Persuasively Toolkit.

This book is about the strategies talented, clever and ambitious academics and researchers need to promote themselves and write persuasively to advance their careers, whether that be through achieving a new position, winning a grant or having your work more widely read. I will show you why you need to make time to write, so you can write well using the strategies I give you. You will be persuading your readers that your research matters. You'll soon be moving from an academic writer to a persuasive writer, taking your place as a commanding authority and making an impact on the world with your research.

Let's get started ...

Part I
The importance of you and your research

CHAPTER 1

Articulating why your research matters

YOU ARE AN EXPERT IN YOUR FIELD

If you want to succeed in academia, you must persuade others your research matters. That means learning to write persuasively, winning publication in journals, gaining promotion and succeeding in your funding applications. That's what this book is all about.

When I talk about academia, I'm including all the people at a university, from professors to students who spend their time researching and engaging in education and learning. Research is a role or activity fundamental to your successful career and requires a systematic process that you, as researchers and academics, use to investigate a problem or topic. When I think about success for you, I mean publishing in quality journals, winning funding for more research, and being promoted. It is having as many people as possible read your work and being changed because of it. This success comes from writing persuasively. This book is about learning persuasive writing skills so you can convince others that your research matters, that your research presents a solution to a problem. I'm not talking about how you do your research or where you publish it. Success means knowing and implementing the writing strategies that will persuade others.

I want to reinforce in this chapter that your research *does* matter. You probably feel you are an expert in your space, or that you know how to write and have already established why your research matters. But perhaps change may not be happening as you would like. So, perhaps you are not communicating as well as you think? I've watched many promising careers falter because talented and clever academics and researchers didn't know how to promote themselves or write persuasively to advance their careers.

YOUR RESEARCH MATTERS

In this chapter we will look at why research matters and the substantial value it delivers to society, including:

- creating knowledge
- driving change
- promoting critical thinking
- helping you to develop your empathy skills.

To succeed in your academic career you have to be an expert in why research matters *and* your research topic. When you add your research to the global pool and it's used by intelligent researchers everywhere, and they create more knowledge, the impact will be greater than the sum of the parts. Research also teaches critical thinking. Those who read your work and follow you are inoculating society against the misinformation that is so widely distributed today.

Research is fundamental to your life and career as an academic. The outputs of your work create knowledge for further research, provide solutions for society and enable change to advance humanity. But researchers need to write well and persuasively to have that impact.

Perhaps you didn't realise that writing and developing your writing skills is crucial to achieving change. Your research matters to you and helps many others. It delivers tremendous value to society, as all research does. Publishing your research is fundamental to a flourishing career. It matters to your success that you publish in high-quality journals and have as many people as possible read your work and be influenced by it. To have this impact, you need to write persuasively. Writing persuasively means convincing others your research matters and presents a solution to a problem, perhaps a novel approach to solving that problem. Writing persuasively means you have strategies to convince others of your argument. Publishing in a range of places means you have more opportunities to persuade people, somewhere on this planet, with your solution.

You may feel you already know how to write well because you've written a PhD. Or, you didn't realise that continuing to write was so important to achieving change in your area. It might feel like you're not being heard – that you lack influence. You may be receiving negative feedback on your articles, with many revisions, or perhaps you are being turned down on your funding applications. You might feel overwhelmed with the amount of research and writing, and the tight deadlines you always work to. Perhaps you run out of time to write well or persuasively. Fundamentally, you need to persuade others. So why do you struggle to get started, and why do you always have writing last on your to-do list?

Professor Carola Vinuesa was studying lupus and other auto-immune diseases at the John Curtin School of Medical Research in Canberra in August 2018, when she received a call from a former student telling her about the Kathleen Folbigg case. When she started to investigate, she teamed up with then-fellow Australian National University immunologist Todor Arsov to chart Folbigg's DNA in the hopes of identifying any mutated genes that might explain a genetic susceptibility for sudden infant deaths.

Over the next several years, Professor Vinuesa led a large team of genetic scientists from across the world, eventually finding that Folbigg carried a mutant gene known as CALM2-G114R – the likely cause of the death of her two daughters. These results lead to Folbigg's release, and when speaking to ABC News Breakfast Professor Vinuesa said, 'As a scientist, you don't always get to do things that really make a difference in someone's life.'

No-one cares about your research as much as you do

No-one cares about your research as much as you do. You need to persuade your readers, assessors and editors to care if you want to achieve change. Research delivers a lot of value to society, and you are one of those researchers. I've seen researchers' careers go stellar once they understand how to promote themselves and their research. For example, let's meet Helen …

> Helen's research on paediatric respiratory disease has been translated into seven clinical guidelines for asthma management worldwide. Her research has also been included in the Global Initiative for Asthma, a medical organisation

that works with public health officials and healthcare professionals globally to reduce asthma prevalence, morbidity and mortality. She now aims to trial her approach with First Nations pregnant women in Australia, whose asthma is more likely to flare up when pregnant.

Helen knows her research matters, and she has learned how to write about it well. If she addresses the needs of her 'users' and writes persuasively about her solution, she can change the health of people with asthma around the world. Before Helen published her research and solution, these people had uncontrolled asthma and a decreased quality of life.

Helen is only one example of how research delivers significant value to society. She shows how confidence and competence can persuade governments and health authorities that research does matter, impacts society and helps the health of many people.

Here's an activity for you. Think about two research problems you've investigated and the solutions you've created. Now list all the groups whose lives would improve if people understood your research. Think outside the box. For example, if your research is about the role of grasshoppers in growing corn, it would help corn farmers, makers of breakfast cereal, world health groups, makers of agricultural equipment, and eaters of breakfast cereal – not to mention the grasshoppers!

You may not have fully thought through who will benefit from your research. Talk it through with a colleague. Ask them how they see your research helping. Sometimes your research might be niche and you need to catch up with how it helps others. It could be part of a bigger whole. Take time to discuss who you help and who benefits from your research.

YOUR RESEARCH CREATES KNOWLEDGE

Research creates knowledge others can use and apply, and when you create knowledge you generate new ideas. You create new arguments that differ from the way people currently think or do things. Creating knowledge comes from the process of testing and building new ideas. You may even establish a new field of research.

Not all of your research has to create large bodies of new knowledge – I'm talking about being super aware of the new knowledge you *are* contributing and then writing about it to persuade others. It might feel like you're only 'doing your work', but any new knowledge you create is important. It contributes to a greater pool of information that others can use and apply. Your research outcomes impact a range of people in society, and you establish your credibility by publishing this new knowledge.

Recently, on a writing retreat, I worked with a team of researchers. They were working towards a funding proposal, and were having trouble articulating the outcomes of their research.

Their first draft included only three outcomes from their research. I then showed them my 'magic table', which shows how to align your research question with your professional aims and outcomes (see chapter 7). They used this table to establish each item they produced from each action of their research. This created an expanded list of 10 outcomes, and they immediately recognised the added value, extent and impact of their research. Their writing flowed after that.

And they submitted their proposal for funding on time. This was after thinking they couldn't get a significant document written and submitted in the allotted period.

At the time of writing they had not heard whether they were successful. But they did use some of what was drafted and the principles of persuasive writing they learned during the retreat to apply for a small internal grant, and were successful.

Consider all the people who will benefit from the knowledge your research creates. Not only other researchers or other universities, but society at large.

You might think, *my outcomes are in a narrow field or are not so valuable*, or *my outcomes only make sense in the university's context*. You still have to explain to the university why your research matters. You still have to explain how it makes a difference to other researchers in your field, and solves a problem of the planet. And you still need to consider the new mantra of whether your research is industry relevant. In spending time articulating what you produce, you can better explain your outcomes and identify the benefits of these to the outside world.

YOUR RESEARCH IMPACTS WIDER SOCIETY AND ACHIEVES CHANGE

Research impacts wider society and achieves change. Your research makes a difference to other researchers in your field. It changes the way society thinks when they know about meaningful outcomes, such as new vaccinations or cures for chronic diseases, or social and cultural outcomes. It's not narrowly about what your research is about or your research topic, it's about who your research is ultimately for and the benefits your research provides them. These are the people who need your research and may pay you for it. You need to be able to articulate the obvious benefits and impacts your research is having on society. Never lose sight of who will benefit.

Think about Branka's work in atmospheric aerosols. Understanding their sources, composition and evolution in the atmosphere is critical. This had been the focus of Branka's approach to writing about her research. She hadn't considered how her research could have an extensive impact until she learned to write persuasively about the development of strategies and policies that improve air quality, public health and the accuracy of climate models. This impacts every person on the planet – and most of us are not interested in aerosols at all.

Your research does impact wider society, and others need to know about it. You might think our world is in information overload and wonder how you can stand out in the crowd. You can stand out in the crowd by becoming good at persuasive writing.

You might feel it's fantastic for Branka to be in the research field of climate change, a topic everyone cares about. But you are focusing on teeth and everyone is less excited about the dentist. You might struggle because you think you're not quite expert enough, or your research isn't as crucial as ensuring women are safe in childbirth. But you still have to name the outputs you will produce from your research. Even if you believe your field is not as glamourous or high profile as some, you still have to identify and write about the impact you want to have to maintain or advance your career. And even if your research will not affect every person on the planet, there is still an audience out there of people who will benefit from your work.

YOUR RESEARCH TEACHES CRITICAL THINKING

Research teaches critical thinking, and we desperately need a dose. You start with a high level of curiosity and ask questions. You engage in analysing, evaluating and creating (as shown in the following image). You conduct a thorough and rigorous test of an idea to see the outcome. Each time you do this, you're pushing your brain to the next level. You also progress society and make people think more, and more critically.

I'm not talking about remembering information or understanding and applying that information. I'm talking about higher order thinking, the critical thinking demanded by your research to solve problems. You are both doing this thinking yourself and encouraging others to do so. We don't want to have the uninformed taking over the world. You need to be good at persuasive writing to overcome the uninformed voices. I will show you how.

Research and writing about your research require
higher order thinking skills

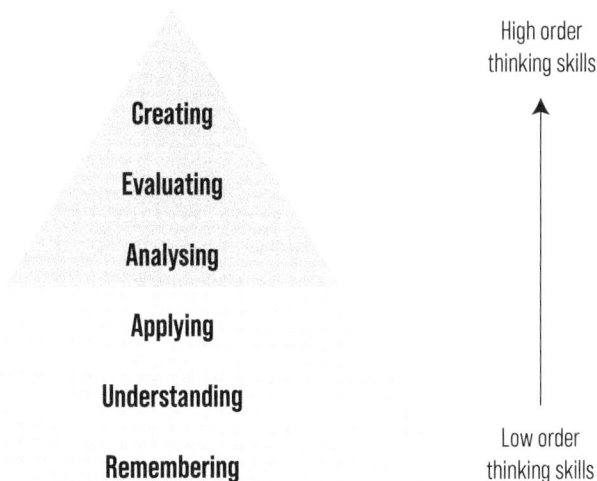

- **Remembering:** recalling information by recognising, listing, describing, retrieving, naming, finding.

- **Understanding:** explaining ideas or concepts, interpreting, summarising, paraphrasing, classifying. When you use the word *summarise* you tell your readers there are **no** new ideas, results or solutions.

- **Applying:** using information in another familiar situation by implementing, carrying out (conducting is a better word because you never use two words when one will do), using, executing.

- **Analysing:** breaking information into parts to explore, understanding and relationships by comparing, organising, deconstructing, interrogating, attributing, outlining, finding, 'constructing', integrating.

- **Evaluating:** justifying a decision or course of action by checking, hypothesising, critiquing, experimenting, judging, testing, detecting, monitoring.

- **Creating:** generating new ideas, products or ways of viewing things by designing, constructing, planning, producing, inventing, devising.

Your work provides a dose of critical thinking we need. Readers and assessors are always looking for a novel idea and approach. Sit back and imagine you have achieved the things you want to achieve with your research. A world with greenhouse gas emissions reduced by 50%? No more shark deaths? No more concussions in contact sports?

Write three paragraphs on how that success would make you feel. You may feel the hurdles to success are too high or you cannot find a mentor to guide you through the maze. You need to imagine success because the world will be better off because of your work – if you can communicate it well.

YOUR RESEARCH DEVELOPS EMPATHY SKILLS

Research develops your empathy skills and that's a substantial personal benefit. By empathy skills, I mean understanding the people who need your research. You need to consider how the 'users' of your research will benefit. I'm not talking about sympathising and being moved by the thoughts and feelings of others. I'm talking about what moves you about the research you have done and the people you have helped.

Reflect for a moment. Who you are researching for? How do you feel when you see how people's lives change because of your research? What about the social and personal benefits when you invent a tool for broken limbs that is free from hospital-associated infections?

> Major discoveries arise when you understand who needs your research and when you feel strongly about the pain they are in and how you can fix this. But promoting your research is just as important, because without strong communication skills your research will not reach the people who need it. Take Karin, for example. She's designing wearable devices for children who have cancer to more accurately measure and describe their levels of pain.

You might think, *I don't need empathy to undertake my research. I am an expert in my field.* You might say you cannot be distracted from your research to focus on the end user. But understanding who needs your research and why will give you important information to do your research. It will make you a better researcher and a better expert.

CONCLUSION

In this chapter, I have reminded you of the social and personal benefits of your role as a researcher and academic. Stop thinking you don't have time to define who you are as a researcher. Stop thinking you don't have time to establish who will benefit from your research and why. Before you launch into your next research project, start promoting research in general, and *your* research benefits in particular. This is the real gig.

In the next chapter, I will show you the first step of that exciting process – stepping into and establishing your researcher identity.

Never heard of a researcher identity? Keep reading.

CHAPTER 1 ACTIVITIES

Here's an activity for you. Think about two research problems you've investigated and the solutions you've created. Now list all the groups whose lives would improve if people understood your research. Think outside the box. For example, if your research is about the role of grasshoppers in growing corn, it would help corn farmers, makers of breakfast cereal, world health groups, makers of agricultural equipment, and eaters of breakfast cereal – not to mention the grasshoppers!

You may not have fully thought through who will benefit from your research. Talk it through with a colleague. Ask them how they see your research helping. Sometimes your research might be niche and you need to catch up with how it helps others. It could be part of a bigger whole. Take time to discuss who you help and who benefits from your research.

*

Your work provides a dose of critical thinking we need. Readers and assessors are always looking for a novel idea and approach. Sit back and imagine you have achieved the things you want to achieve with your research. A world with greenhouse gas emissions reduced by 50%? No more shark deaths? No more concussions in contact sports?

Write three paragraphs on how that success would make you feel. You may feel the hurdles to success are too high or you cannot find a mentor to guide you through the maze. You need to imagine success because the world will be better off because of your work – if you can communicate it well.

CHAPTER 2

Why your researcher identity matters

LETTING PEOPLE KNOW YOU AND YOUR WORK EXIST

This step of thinking about your researcher identity and why it matters is so often overlooked. Every researcher creates an identity as they work in their field. You need to be in control of it and be able to articulate it. You need to stand out. That is what this chapter is all about.

Writing is a lot of thinking. The actual job to be done is letting people know you and your work exist.

Here you can address your concern about identity. The first step is to find out where you are now, what your current researcher identity is and whether you are happy with it. (In chapter 4, I'll show you how to establish a strong researcher identity.)

What is a researcher identity? It is your unique set of characteristics that defines you as a researcher and makes you different from other researchers. It's your brand within your field, the area of knowledge in which you conduct your research. Is it structural engineering, neuroscience, health equity, human rights law, personal narratives in creating social change, applied economics or symmetric cryptology?

Taking control of your researcher identity means being the one who decides where and when you confidently state your identity. Have it defined, and refined. Have it ready to present at any time. You're not identifying your personal characteristics or describing what you do each day. I'm talking about how you want to be perceived as a researcher, and how you position yourself in your field or in your body of knowledge. It is also about where and why you belong in this field. Your researcher identity is your expertise and what makes you valuable to your field or your university. The same applies to commercial researchers investigating a problem and writing about a solution for a client. It's about your vision.

You might think you have established an identity, or are too early in your career to have an identity. But you can manage and change how you are perceived as a researcher just by articulating that you are an expert in your field. Writing this well is critical. Every researcher needs to stand out from the crowd to advance their career.

Janice has done this. Here's her researcher identity:

> Janice's cutting-edge approaches and knowledge of Design for All with co-design expertise and expertise in the GLAM (galleries, libraries, archives and museums) sector, recognise the importance of rethinking access and inclusion for people with disabilities – not as an add-on but as central to understanding the public and economic roles of the GLAM sector and of culture and tourism

more widely. Her inclusive design is an integral element of Australian and international recognition of what equal rights for people living with disabilities means.

The assessors in her grant proposal perceived Janice as a researcher who had clearly established her researcher identity. They described her as an accomplished researcher who should be supported to continue her important research. Her unusual combination of disciplinary skills makes her one of the few people in Australia to take up the challenges identified, and her commitment is clear. You must make sure you clearly define yourself as a researcher in your field. Take control of it. Stand out from the crowd, just as Janice did to receive funding for her important research.

In this chapter, I'm going to establish why your researcher identity is critical for your success. We'll start the process by making sure you know exactly how you are perceived – which is harder than you think.

A WELL-DEFINED AND MEMORABLE IDENTITY

Your researcher identity must be at hand for you to use everywhere. Everywhere means in the articles you publish and the funding documents you write, and at all the speaking gigs that come your way. It needs to be on your university websites and in your brochures and bios. I define researcher identity as *your unique set of characteristics that identifies you as a researcher and makes you different from other researchers*. It's the words you use to define your unique wow factor. It's not about listing what you do in your daily activities as a researcher, but questioning whether people fully understand your expertise and what it is you stand for. I'm talking about articulating that you are an expert in your field and then writing this down.

Thinking about these characteristics and your expertise is hard. And writing it often gets you tangled. This is true for all of us. We all struggle with writing about ourselves, within academia and in industry. Understanding what is unique about us is a difficult proposition. Later I'm going to explain the step-by-step process of how to do it.

> Others recognise your capacity as a researcher based on what you tell them. Tatheer, an early career structural engineer, presented her achievements at the QUT Women in Research showcase event. Her brand and ambitious research agenda to use sustainable 3D-printed reinforcing materials to replace conventional carbon-intensive materials in construction was very strong. So strong, the registrar approached her following the presentation, offering funding and resources.

> You need to have your researcher identity ready, and then articulate it so you can persuade others of your value, just like Tatheer could. This amplified her status and enabled her to take advantage of that five-minute research speaking opportunity that came her way. You might think people judge you on your research alone. Sure, your research does matter, but how you talk about yourself and your research, to create your identity, is the number one thing.

Think of the last networking event you attended. How did it go when you introduced yourself and explained who you are as a researcher? If you can't remember the last time, introduce yourself to a colleague as if you are meeting them for the first time. How did you go with this introduction? Were you happy? Was it succinct? Was it powerful, or did you stumble over words?

What would you think of these researchers when they introduce themselves?

I am an expert in plant genetic engineering and agricultural biotechnology, with my ultimate goal being to develop major cultivated crops with better resilience to environmental stresses caused by pests and diseases.

I am an Australian constitutional law scholar, exploring the scope and limits of the powers that can be exercised by the Federal Executive Council, clarifying the legal principles governing the relationship between legislation and executive power.

As a professional musician and teacher, I develop entrepreneurial competencies in young people to enter the professional music industry. For example, I created Australia's first university record label, Vermilion Records, managed by students across music, film, entertainment, creative writing, marketing and design.

You may think it is your research that persuades others, not what you say. Most of us can be more succinct and elegant in how we describe ourselves and our research. It is something we all struggle with and it can be embarrassing. But you know what? I, and many others, won't be interested in your research if you don't have a well-defined and memorable identity.

EXPLORING YOUR RESEARCHER IDENTITY

You already have a researcher identity, even if you don't realise it. We all have a brand, regardless of whether we have consciously created it. Later, I'm going to show you how to shape that brand, but first, I'm going to give you clues on how to find out what is unique about you and how you differ from other researchers in your field.

Establishing how you want people to think about you is the first step. You need to establish a unique factor and a differentiator:

- **Unique factors** are the notable personal attributes, and life and professional experiences, that make you different from those in your field or in your team.

- **Differentiators** show the difference between your expertise and that of your colleagues and competitors in your field; the notable methodology, methods, approach and theories you use that make you different. It's about how you position yourself in your body of knowledge or your field of research. It is critical you define your differentiator and then articulate it to others, so they fully understand your differentiator and why it's so important.

I'm not talking about listing what you do in your daily activities as a researcher or the projects you are involved in. What's important is the information in your identity and articulating how you want to be perceived as a researcher so others fully understand your expertise. What you stand for is the key here. Your identity is what gets you out of bed each day. It's what drives you to find the solutions to the problems you investigate. You might think that everybody knows you, that you know how others perceive you. But you can't know if your researcher identity is working for you until you know what it is. Have you written down your researcher identity?

A few years back I was working with an academic, developing her researcher identity for her promotion documents. It was clear she was an international leader in design robotics. I did not know or understand for some time that she was not a designer, a roboticist or a digital something or other. In fact, she was an architect working at the cutting edge of architectural thinking. Nowhere in her researcher identity had she clearly articulated the foundation of her brand, even though her identity as an architect was important to her.

As an expert, you know your research inside out. You need to be prepared to work hard to show your uniqueness. And you can't rush this. It's important you allocate time to write it. And then you need to tell everyone. You might think branding is inauthentic, or perhaps you hate talking about yourself, but you need to get past this to properly promote yourself and your work. You need to find a way to say how great you are that doesn't sound like bragging, that focuses on your best and unique attributes and sounds sincere and powerful.

Let's look at how you perceive yourself as a researcher. How do you define your expertise and explain how you are unique? Conduct your own research about yourself this time. Find what you already have about your identity. Search through your biographies on the university website, and the profiles you have written for conferences, articles, or when you were a keynote or guest speaker.

While you are doing this research about yourself, collect the examples that best tell your story. Put them in one place, a folder on your computer called 'My researcher identity'. You will need this information when you get to chapter 4.

How confident are you that you can promote your uniqueness and expertise succinctly? And at any time and any place? Have a read of the information you collected in the reflection activity above. Is this the best way to present yourself and your research to the world?

ESTABLISHING HOW OTHERS SEE YOU

You need to establish how others perceive you as a researcher and an expert in your field. Ask people you already know how they think about you as a researcher. Can they identify and say what makes you unique and different from the rest? This step is about finding out what others think. It can be difficult, and even embarrassing. It is valuable, though, because others often say great things about you, things that are more flattering and positive than you would say about yourself.

You may feel how others perceive you is not that important. But is what they think and say accurate? Does it correctly reflect who you are as a researcher? Does it accurately present what you stand for and your vision? Is your story succinctly articulated so others will fully understand your unique researcher identity?

Consider how accurately defining your researcher identity will engage more industry bodies and others outside your area of expertise. You need to control how others perceive you and your research, which means crafting your statement and your identity well. Once you have a good understanding of your researcher identity, you can confidently present yourself in your biography, elevator speech, articles, grant applications, promotion documents and presentations.

Then you will get the recognition you deserve. You need your researcher identity story right now. It is critical to being understood, and for being published, funded and promoted.

Investigate how others see you and how others perceive you as a researcher. How do they explain how you are unique and define your expertise? Put your researcher hat on again. Ask three different people you know how they would introduce you if you were the keynote speaker at their next conference.

Ask them if you can record what they say. Use an app that transcribes their words. You might find some pearls. Or you might be aghast at how little they can accurately say about your researcher identity. This might highlight how much work you need to do to establish and clearly articulate your researcher identity.

Keep these recordings. You will need them in chapter 4. If you can't see the urgency of defining or establishing your researcher identity, imagine what will happen when the world knows how unique and expert you are and why your research matters.

CONCLUSION

In this chapter, you have learned that every researcher needs to create an identity and articulate it succinctly and powerfully. To be successful, you need to stand out. How exciting will it be when you confidently articulate your unique set of characteristics that establishes you as a researcher who is different from all the others? You will benefit when others can present you, and your researcher identity, accurately to the rest of the world.

Stop saying you will get to establishing your identity when you write your next publication or your next document. Start here. Start now. Reflect on your uniqueness as a researcher and what makes you different from others in your field and your research team. These ideas all lead to the exciting step in chapter 4 when you will complete your wording about your researcher identity.

Now you know the value and criticality of establishing your researcher identity. In the next chapter, I will show you how to shift from an academic writer to an effective persuasive writer and achieve an impact. You can read how Elizabeth followed this writing process and moved from an adequate to an excellent writer and communicator – someone who is publishing more and receiving more rewards, grants, contracts and other opportunities than she ever imagined she could achieve.

CHAPTER 2 ACTIVITIES

Let's look at how you perceive yourself as a researcher. How do you define your expertise and explain how you are unique? Conduct your own research about yourself this time. Find what you already have about your identity. Search through your biographies on the university website, and the profiles you have written for conferences, articles, or when you were a keynote or guest speaker.

While you are doing this research about yourself, collect the examples that best tell your story. Put them in one place, a folder on your computer called 'My researcher identity'. You will need this information when you get to chapter 4.

*

Investigate how others see you and how others perceive you as a researcher. How do they explain how you are unique and define your expertise? Put your researcher hat on again. Ask three different people you know how they would introduce you if you were the keynote speaker at their next conference.

Ask them if you can record what they say. Use an app that transcribes their words. You might find some pearls. Or you might be aghast at how little they can accurately say about your researcher identity. This might highlight how much work you need to do to establish and clearly articulate your researcher identity.

Keep these recordings. You will need them in chapter 4. If you can't see the urgency of defining or establishing your researcher identity, imagine what will happen when the world knows how unique and expert you are and why your research matters.

CHAPTER 3

Why writing to achieve impact matters

SHIFTING FROM ACADEMIC WRITER TO PERSUASIVE WRITER

This chapter is about the shift from being an academic writer to an effective persuasive writer. Persuasive writing is a way of achieving impact. Effective persuasive writing is writing that shows your capacity and competency while persuading others of your value and expertise. Your academic writing can also be persuasive writing. It's not that one is the wrong sort of writing, but understanding persuasive writing and academic writing will help you make the shift. I'm going to give you a diagnostic tool to help you appraise where you are now, and introduce you to the persuasive writing process and what to do to become a super-powerful researcher.

Branka had an epiphany with her approach to writing during our writing retreat. As a scientist, she depends on facts and usually lets them speak for themselves. But this time she wrote to persuade the readers of her funding proposal to give her money. She wanted to persuade them her research will identify the Southern Ocean aerosols and the impact on cloud formation and climate.

Shifting means changing the way you write about your research. Your responsibility is to publish and communicate with the world about your research, to write about the benefits of your research so people understand the difference you make to society economically, environmentally, culturally or with new knowledge. I want to change the way you think about persuasive writing. I'm not talking about writing the way you have always written your articles and documents, as if they are a report. I'm talking about engaging with your research and its benefits, establishing your story and convincing others you have important research that can change lives.

You might feel you are well published and doing okay, but if your aim is to position yourself as a leading researcher and a voice of authority, you need to change the way you present your research. You need to write a powerful argument for why your research matters. 'Doing okay' will not make you stand out in your field.

Imagine your success when you have persuaded more people to understand your research and act on it. If you write for other academics or people in your field, they are already interested in your topic. Persuasive writing is for different audiences. I want you to understand the distinction, not feel that one is wrong.

Consider Marianella, an industrial design researcher who knows how important different perspectives are to innovation and success. She has harnessed her passion to design and create better healthcare technology and solve problems as a female researcher. Now a professor, Marianella has learned to write persuasively and to engage a wider audience. She is winning funding and being supported by government and industry.

This knowledge and these skills are not innate. They are learned. It has taken her time. To position yourself as a leading researcher, a voice of authority, you need to start now. Learn the skill of writing persuasively and write a powerful argument for why your research matters.

In this chapter, we'll examine what persuasive writing means, how it differs from other types of writing, and introduce *The Five-Step Writing Framework* you will use later in this book to master this essential skill.

PERSUASIVE WRITING CHANGES READERS' MINDS

Persuasive writing changes readers' minds and shows your competency and capacity. Let's explore what persuasive writing means by comparing academic and persuasive writing.

Academic writing	Persuasive writing
Presents evidence.	Presents an argument.
For a particular, formal audience or your community. Aims to extend the group's knowledge or to initiate new members into the group.	Is all about the reader. Considers all audiences. Aims to shape people's beliefs or lead your reader to action.

Academic writing	Persuasive writing
Centres on a main topic.	Depends on arguments that 'rely on a range of appeals'. In your case as a researcher, these arguments are based on: • logic and evidence • a range of audiences • your creditability.
Often looks like a report of what you have done.	Writer steps back from the research to: • conceptualise it • assert and support a viable claim.
Moves the reader from what is known to what is new.	Grounded in arguments intended to change the audiences' beliefs or actions.
Values logical argument and critical reflection.	Demonstrates higher order critical thinking. Starts with how you critique the sources you cite. Uses specific verbs (see following table) that enhance your argument, e.g. analysing and evaluating and creating new ideas or ways of viewing things by designing, constructing, planning, producing, inventing, devising.

Verbs to use when presenting an argument		
Analysing	Evaluating	Creating
Distinguish	Judge	Compose
Question	Rate	Assemble
Appraise	Validate	Organise
Experiment	Predict	Invent
Inspect	Assess	Compile
Examine	Score	Forecast
Probe	Revise	Devise
Separate	Infer	Propose
Inquire	Determine	Construct
Arrange	Prioritise	Plan
Investigate	Compare	Prepare
Sift	Evaluate	Develop
Compare	Defend	Originate
Contrast	Select	Imagine
Survey	Measure	Generate
Detect	Choose	Formulate
Group	Conclude	Improve
Order	Deduce	Act
Sequence	Debate	Predict
Test	Justify	Produce
Debate	Recommend	Blend
Analyse	Discriminate	Set up
Diagram	Appraise	Concoct
Relate	Value	
Research	Probe	
Dissect	Argue	
Calculate	Decide	
Criticise	Rank	
Categorise	Reject	
Discriminate	Dispute	

Persuasive writers change the way they think about their readers. They consider what their readers want to read and hear about, and why. I'm not saying that academic writing is not persuasive, but it's persuasive for a particular audience. You need to be able to write for many other kinds of audiences as well. Consider your reader and what they need to read if they are going to act on what you write and change the way they think. You might think this sounds like hard work – and you would be right. Writing persuasively means you need to provide the right information in the right way for people to make decisions. You need to give them your message in a manner that they will receive it and act on it.

Few researchers understand the distinction between academic and persuasive writing. Many mistake 'persuasive' for 'salesy'. But the distinction is about extending your ability to write – a honing of your skills. Persuasive writing targets your niche audiences who each have different concerns. It won't leave your work on the shelf. You're an incredible thinker and you know you've produced something meaningful. What you're trying to do is remind your audiences you've produced something meaningful, and change people's minds.

Think for a moment about writing for a grant. What is going to persuade the people who give you money for your research? It will differ from writing an article, or for *The Conversation*, or for a podcast. You are writing for different audiences. There can be many variations, even within academic audiences, especially with transdisciplinary research today. You must consider the reader and what they need to hear.

> Consider Chaturanga's success. Chaturanga has been working to significantly advance the current level of understanding of the bactericidal mechanism of nanopillar

topography. He is developing a suite of novel methodologies that measure the metabolic activity of bacteria. You may wonder what this research is all about because it is complex and difficult to understand. Do you think this complexity was helpful for his grant applications?

Because he rephrased how he describes his work– establishing for the first time in the world a biomaterial that will stop infection on implants, those metal rods you have inserted when you break a bone – his latest grant proposal scored 99.4 out of 100. They awarded him funding based on the three criteria of excellence, impact and implementation. It's not easy to persuade readers that your research is amazing and will solve a real-world problem – in this case, infection prevention for biomedical applications. It requires effort to change people's minds.*

You might think Chaturanga is a researcher who writes only for the scientific community. And you might think this writing is a specialist skill. Or you might think this is not within your capability. All researchers need to persuade their target audiences. In Chaturanga's case, he has to persuade the scientific audience, other researchers, funding bodies, medical institutes such as industrial developers of these new biomaterials, and public audiences.

Reflect on a time persuasive writing or persuasive messages have influenced you and changed your mind about a topic or idea; for example, same-sex marriage or the Uluru Statement from the Heart.

---

* If you want to achieve this kind of result, join my next writing retreat. Go to klgcommunications.com.au for more information.

If you are struggling to think of examples, consider researchers in your field you have critiqued who had different views or ways of going about research that is like yours.

What have you written that persuades others your research is valuable and has an impact?

IF IT MATTERS TO YOU, WHY DO YOU STRUGGLE TO PERSUADE OTHERS?

No-one cares as much about your research as you do – until you make them care. But if it matters to you, why do you struggle to persuade people about the value of your work? You *can* achieve change. As I mentioned in chapter 1, one PhD does not make a career in academia. When you can make others care, you will have a greater impact. It's easy to think your mother, partner, family, colleagues and supervisor are your world. It's easy to believe they care as much as you and that you are surrounded by people who are interested in what you are doing. But you are the only person who really knows your passion, your drive and your commitment to spending years thinking long and hard about how to solve a complex problem and improve people's lives to make the world a better place.

Persuading others about the benefits of your research and making yourself accountable for your research effort is the answer to having an impact. It's not that people don't care – they do – but you care *more*. That's the distinction. You know more about the value and benefits of your research. If you write well about your work, you can get people up to your level with almost the same burning passion. This might feel like you're pushing uphill, but in chapter 1 we looked at how important research is and how important *your* research is. When you understand the idea that no-one cares as much about your research as you do, you will know how hard you have to work on your writing to make others care and see the value in your work.

> Rachel is an early career researcher. She realised no-one would care about her research unless she persuaded them. Rachel set out to do that by announcing her latest publication on LinkedIn. She highlighted the new knowledge she created and provided free access to the article. Like an increasing number of researchers, Rachel now has the power of social media behind her. You might think a huge number of people feel as passionate about your research as you do because you're in climate change, international law or international design forums. However, how sure are you?

Consider this – have you ever *asked* who cares about your work? Try asking 10 people to rate how much they care about your research topic compared with three burning topics such as climate change, the cost of living and the Uluru Statement from the Heart. It's better to know if people don't care about your work – then you know you have to persuade them.

INFLUENTIAL WRITING IS A SUPERPOWER FOR RESEARCHERS

When you think about it, influential writing is a superpower for academics. It will help you achieve the impact you are after to change people's minds and persuade them your research matters.

How would you rate yourself for this superpower? Try this diagnostic to rate where you are now. Rate the time you currently spend in each stage of the writing process.

Time you currently spend in each stage of the writing process		
The steps	Percentage of your allocated writing time you currently spend on each step to produce a document.	How much do you prioritise each step? e.g. low, medium, high, not at all.
1. Think		
2. Read		
3. Plan		
4. Write		
5. Revise		

Source: Write Persuasively Toolkit, klgcommunications.com.au

To make writing a superpower and become a powerful researcher to supercharge your career, you need to practise. It's only in comics that they give superpowers without effort. In the real world, you have to practise every day and book time to write in your calendar. Don't leave your writing to the last minute, just as you tell your students not to do.

One of my clients books time in her calendar to write once a week. Every Friday morning we meet at 8:00, and by 9:00 we have checked her plan for the day and what she is going to write. Then she practises writing until 4:00 pm, working with a group of creative, business and research writers. Through practice, we are aiming to improve – to shift from a writer to a persuasive writer.

You might think, *I couldn't book out that much time in my week.* Why not? What is stopping you? You will get brilliant at this, win more research grants and publications, and then have more money and more time. Consider the message from writing coach Kath Walters in her book *Overnight Authority*. She says writing is 99% momentum.

Ask people if they have ever heard an inspiring person talk. What about Brené Brown, the American professor? She's a great communicator and cares about her research. Writing about it and sharing it with the world is clearly her superpower. Perhaps you've never thought of writing as a superpower. It is – and there's no better time than now, so let's get on with developing it.

THE FIVE-STEP WRITING FRAMEWORK

My writing process that I will share with you now is a five-step framework of thinking, reading, planning, writing and revising – and it's all about time. The point of the framework is to improve the amount of time you spend on writing.

Let's work through the framework now (see overleaf). The writing process is sequential and iterative. Feedback is an important component in each of these steps. We are talking about you going through this process each time you want to produce a document, any document – *every* document.

The Five-Step Writing Framework goes from planning to publication. Thousands of researchers at universities and people in industry have tried and tested it over the years, in Australia and in Europe. The process gets you ready to start writing for a specific purpose.

The Five-Step Writing Framework

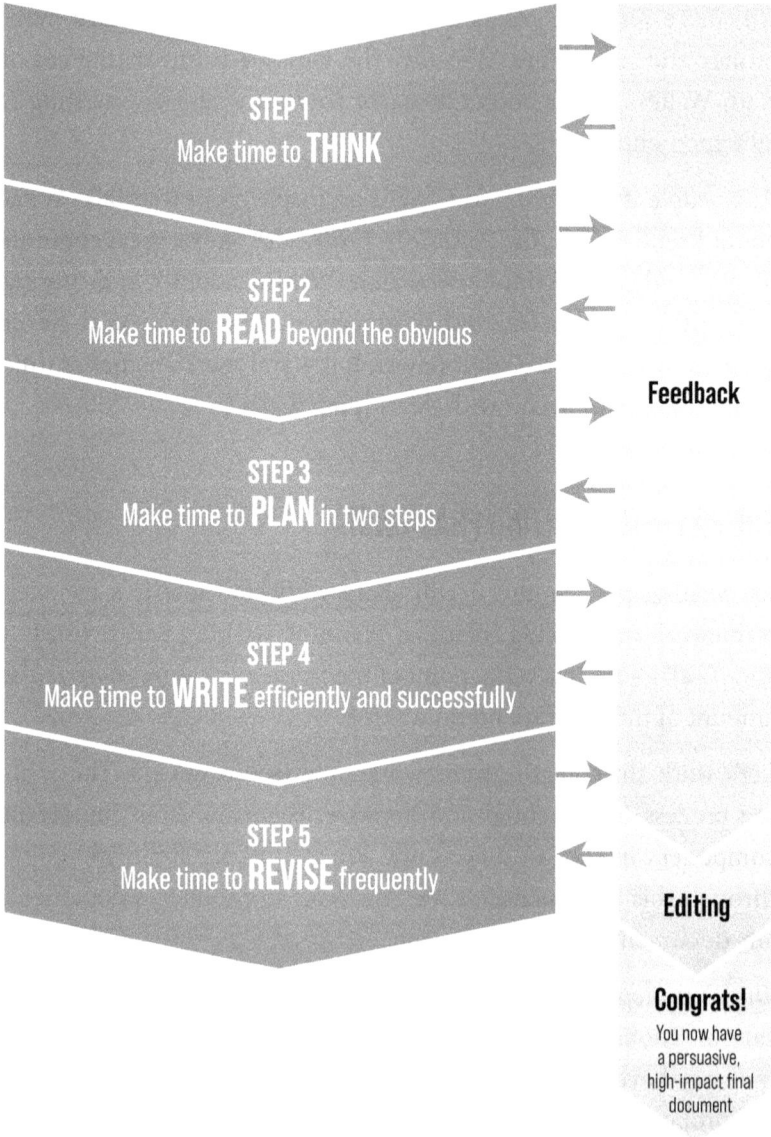

STEP 1
Make time to **THINK**

STEP 2
Make time to **READ** beyond the obvious

STEP 3
Make time to **PLAN** in two steps

STEP 4
Make time to **WRITE** efficiently and successfully

STEP 5
Make time to **REVISE** frequently

Feedback

Editing

Congrats!
You now have
a persuasive,
high-impact final
document

Source: Write Persuasively Toolkit, klgcommunications.com.au

You start by making time to think about what you are going to write. Then you get feedback from a variety of people about your thinking process before you move on to the next step: reading. Once you have done some fundamental activities here, you check in again and get feedback before you move on to the planning step. This is an exciting step because the amount of time you spend here will save you so much time in the long run and give you a persuasive document. It's important to get feedback again – from different people – before you start writing. And starting to write looks like pages of dot points before you move on to writing in sentences. Fundamental to the entire process is getting feedback at each of these steps.

Knowing, understanding and following this writing process will shift you from an academic writer to an effective persuasive writer – and we have already established what this means for you. The tremendous benefit of knowing that writing is a process is that you can put it into practice. You can work through each of the steps and apply the process to all your writing tasks.

> The writing process is not complicated, but it still requires effort. Let's look at how Katharina started with the writing process. Katharina left her industry to undertake a PhD. She had been designing therapeutic gardens in hospitals around the world for many years. She knew the health benefits of her designs and wanted these design principles established as a policy. Her aim is for every new hospital built to have a therapeutic garden, and every hospital retrofitted to include a therapeutic garden.

> Katharina was an expert at writing design briefs but she knew little about academic writing or writing to persuade her readers, or writing for different audiences. Her audiences

now include government at all levels and health executives, design researchers, academics and landscape architects.

We met at the start of her research journey, so she has followed the writing process and all of its steps from day one. She was lucky to start fresh. Katharina's success in her two-year journey to date includes publishing articles, winning scholarships and gaining access to the world's leaders in healthcare design.

Knowing, understanding and following the writing process will shift you from a new entrant to the academy to an effective persuasive writer. You might say you've learned a different kind of writing process or you go about your writing differently. There is no one correct way, but if you have learned another way and you're still struggling, try this way.

Look at *The Five-Step Writing Framework* and get ready to develop your writing superpower.

CONCLUSION

In this chapter, you learned you are an incredible thinker, and that no-one cares more about your research than you. Persuasive writing is a way of achieving impact. It is a shift from one kind of writing to the next. Persuasive writing is for different audiences, grounded in arguments intended to change these audiences' beliefs or actions. You also learned that writing is your superpower. When you use it to persuade others about the value and benefits of your research, you will gain respect and success. You have learned about the process of writing. When you use *The Five-Step Writing Framework* of thinking, reading, planning, writing and revising, and increase the amount of time you spend on writing, you will become a respected researcher who is publishing widely, winning funding, being promoted and impacting people's lives and society.

Stop rushing your writing tasks and undervaluing yourself. Writing is all about time. Start putting time in your calendar each day – or at least once a week – to practise your superpower.

You are an ambitious researcher. You know the value of writing to achieve impact and the success that can come your way when you have persuaded more people to listen to you and your ideas. In the next chapter, I will show you the first step of *The Five-Step Writing Framework*. To be a winner, you will follow the five steps, one at a time, in each of the next five chapters.

✒ CHAPTER 3 ACTIVITIES

Reflect on a time persuasive writing or persuasive messages have influenced you and changed your mind about a topic or idea; for example, same-sex marriage or the Uluru Statement from the Heart.

If you are struggling to think of examples, consider researchers in your field you have critiqued who had different views or ways of going about research that is like yours.

What have you written that persuades others your research is valuable and has an impact?

*

How would you rate yourself for this superpower? Try this diagnostic to rate where you are now. Rate the time you currently spend in each stage of the writing process.

Time you currently spend in each stage of the writing process		
The steps	Percentage of your allocated writing time you currently spend on each step to produce a document.	How much do you prioritise each step? e.g. low, medium, high, not at all.
1. Think		
2. Read		
3. Plan		
4. Write		
5. Revise		

Source: Write Persuasively Toolkit, klgcommunications.com.au

Part II
The Five-
Step Writing
Framework

CHAPTER 4

Step 1: Make time to think

SMOOTH THE WAY TO COMPLETION

Writing is a process, and the first step is to make time to think. I don't want you to rush your writing. Taking time at the beginning will smooth your writing process all the way to completion. And, ultimately, your ability to write persuasively will deliver more time into your career. You're going to have more support and more money, and move higher up the ranks. There is always the argument about having no time. The time you dedicate here is time well spent and will save you time later. Start by thinking about yourself as a writer of research.

In chapter 2 we established that, for you to succeed, you must be able to define your researcher identity and how you want to be perceived as a researcher. We are talking about allocating an hour in your calendar every second day for two weeks, to start refining your researcher identity statement. Approach your writing with the mindset of taking the time upfront. Identify and allocate time in your day. Put it in your calendar to stop what you are doing and engage in a specific task of writing.

Take time in this step to think of yourself as a writer of research. For some researchers, this is overlooked. But time is the critical piece missing for success in most writing. Make time in this step before you start writing … well, anything!

When I talk about thinking, I mean a specific type of thinking: the mental process of defining and organising ideas. This is hard for everyone. I'm not talking about 'wandering through the forest' thinking or 'rushing through the supermarket' thinking. This is not 'worrying about getting your writing done by the deadline' thinking, 'relaxing your brain in the shower' thinking or 'finishing off the ironing' thinking. I'm talking about a systematic process of testing your expression of your researcher identity. You might think it's a frivolous task to make time to think about yourself as a writer, but you would be mistaken. Making the time to think about yourself as a writer of research is the first critical step in the writing process. This step needs to be undertaken so others can understand your value as a researcher. Once you understand how it is done, you will see more of its value.

> One of my clients, Karin, has just checked in to update her researcher identity. Having completed two projects over the last year, she now wants to update to her latest and greatest. She wants to stand out from everyone else in her field. She knows the process, and that she must keep it fresh to stay ahead of the game.

Making time to think and define your researcher identity is a critical first step if you are to write effectively about your research. It is this step that sets you apart from everyone else in your field.

Every year, I facilitate a Women in Research writing retreat for 20 women. The feedback I received from one academic is typical of many: 'I have been so exhausted from the semester that whenever I sat down to write, it was an effort. The time and physical space and being part of a group gave me the headspace and energy to focus.' Another academic said, 'It was the earlier part of the writing process where these exercises helped me piece together my thoughts about myself as a researcher and what I wanted my reader to take away from my writing.' Making time to think, in a comfortable physical place, is a critical first step in writing persuasively.

THINKING ABOUT YOUR RESEARCHER IDENTITY

In my workshops where I teach about the writing process, I ask participants to think about their researcher identity – just as I asked you in chapter 2. Thinking is the first part of the writing process. I'm not saying this is easy. It is hard for everyone. But by creating this time, you are adding a step to your entire process of writing that will blow your previous efforts out of the water.

In the workshop, I ask them to turn on their phone and start the record app, swap phones with a colleague and then introduce themselves to their colleague, each taking turns. When they play back their recordings and listen to the way they introduced themselves, these researchers quickly understand the need to have their identity planned, written, refined and ready to present. It's like having your elevator pitch ready. You never know when you need to tell people how unique you are.

Making the time to establish your researcher identity clearly means making time to think about why you are different. There is a difference between your *unique factors* and your *differentiator*.

What about your expertise makes you valuable to the university, now and over the next five years? Yes, this is hard – that is why I've dedicated an entire chapter to it.

Establishing your researcher identity means thinking about your unique factors. These are your personal actions and behaviours that show you are sufficiently different from other researchers. Your professional skills and experiences that relate to your field of research and the subject area you know so much about also need to be defined.

Your differentiator is the elements of your research and expertise that enable a difference or distinction to be made between you and other researchers. In this chapter, we're going to look at differentiators. They are hard, not just in research but in all professions. You need to know what other researchers are doing. You would have established this in your PhD or masters, when you did your literature review. You will also be able to tell by looking at the websites of these other researchers and finding out how they describe themselves today.

Together, your unique factors and differentiator make you valuable. They show you are experienced, and have value and esteem for others to admire and respect you.

The benefits you bring to your research workplace, the university or industry where you work, are your value. It's important for you to think about how you package this information. Establishing your researcher identity, your unique factors and differentiator, will amplify your research status so others will understand your value.

It might seem like a marketing exercise, and in a way, it is. Some people refer to your 'research brand'. This term can feel yucky, so I prefer to use the term 'researcher identity'. You already have a researcher identity and you need to write positively about the value of your identity so you can grow and develop in the modern research university and industry context.

Have a read of and check your identity statement. It defines your reputation and you need to define and control it. Consider how many researchers there are in Australia today.* It's time to think about your identity. Unless you can nail what makes you stand out, you won't gain recognition.

> My colleague Alina has nailed what makes her distinct. She has experience in sustainability, electric vehicles, the circular economy and energy transition from Sydney to Silicon Valley, advising organisations on strategic opportunities in the energy and transport sectors. She's also a researcher, entrepreneur and TEDx presenter.
>
> How do you think she has established her researcher identity? I often use Alina's biography drafts to show how thinking of your identity takes time. Three years ago, we were on version eight. Today, with version 23, she has added value to her reputation, having been precise about why she should be a director of a national energy and climate advisory team.

You might think, *she is more unique or distinct than me, working in a field that is more appealing than mine. Mine is about chemistry and pollution,* or, *I was a nurse before I did my PhD and became an academic, so I'm not as well qualified.* But all your experiences contribute to making you the unique researcher you are today.

---

* Have a look at this website to see how many researchers there are in Australia, and the list of the world's top researchers in their chosen fields identified by public indices: https://campusmorningmail.com.au/news/where-australias-hici-researchers-are-and-why-it-matters/. This article examines the increased significance of multidisciplinary research endeavours across the world and the weakening Western influence.

DEVELOPING YOUR RESEARCHER IDENTITY

Thinking about and selecting which of your experiences and skills best amplifies your profile or identity and status takes time. Writing your value into your best story that amplifies your profile, identity and status takes more time. The following exercise will help you to do this.

Allocate time to do some deep thinking – spend one hour every second day for two weeks. The alternate days give you time to reflect and let your ideas percolate in your brain. Or you might double this allocation, as thinking and writing the answers below does take time.

Prepare to write your researcher identity by answering these questions.

What makes you unique?

Here is an example of a unique point.

> *My years nursing chronic wounds enabled me to develop a risk assessment tool for delayed healing of chronic wounds which predicts with 80% accuracy whether a wound will heal within 24 weeks.*

Here is another example.

> *My real-world experience as a teacher and leader in remote schools means Resource X, which I developed, will build trauma-informed teachers who can support students and address trauma behaviours of children in remote communities.*

Here is an example of another unique point.

> *I examine through the lens of neuroscience the impact of complex trauma – physical, emotional and sexual abuse, serious*

neglect, and family violence – on brain development and functioning, and the school experiences of victims.

Remember your unique point is not the same as your differentiator. Identifying what makes you unique and different from your colleagues is challenging. Your unique point can include personal attributes and experiences. Your differentiator could be the difference between your expertise and that of your colleagues in your field.

What is your differentiator?

Here is an example of a differentiator.

I research stakeholder and community engagement as a relational communication process that aims to build social capital and contribute to civic outcomes.

Here is another example.

I am an expert symmetric (not asymmetric) cryptologist investigating encryption algorithms that use shared secret keys to protect information.

What is it about your uniqueness and differentiator that makes you valuable?

Here is an example.

I am an interaction analyst whose research explores the hidden worlds of children's lives in the home, school and playground. I use video-ethnography and video-stimulated accounts to involve children as analysers of their own experiences, and teacher-researchers to reflect on their own practice. I work with the Department of Education to create professional learning resources for educators that identify effective communicative strategies between educators and children.

My research develops empirically informed teaching strategies that help educators create safe and supportive social environments for learning.

Here is another example.

My unique factor is my national reputation in consumer partnership methods, enabling successful health and medical research that involves consumers. My differentiator (from other consumer behaviour researchers) is my accreditation in Luma design thinking, democratising knowledge that gives people a voice and allows them to be active participants in decision-making processes that affect their lives.

What examples tell your story?

I'm assuming you have a file for all your achievements. Perhaps you have an Excel spreadsheet on your desktop. You can use these examples to illustrate how you and your research are distinct. If you don't have a file, start one immediately!

I like the PepTalkHer app. You can use it to keep track of your career wins and the milestones you hit, and save emails from happy clients and photos of events where you present. This evidence builds your researcher identity. When you keep it up to date, it will surprise you how successful you have been. The PepTalkHer app is suitable for everyone to use.

Keep all the information from this exercise together because you will use it in a moment to craft a complete researcher identity statement.

You might struggle to do this exercise because answering each of these questions can be hard. That is why you need time. When you do it, you will stand out because not everybody puts in the time.

STEP 1: MAKE TIME TO THINK

REFINING YOUR RESEARCHER IDENTITY

In this section, you are going to make time to expand your researcher identity and amplify your status in two ways:

- By making time to think about how you position yourself in your research field. Where and why do you belong in this field? Where are you positioned within your research team?

- By making time to describe your vision. Tune in to what you get out of bed for each day. What drives you? And what do you bring to the research table?

Thinking about where you are positioned means identifying the way you are placed or located within your area of research. This can be tricky when your research field, the area of your research, your body of knowledge and your scientific community are multidisciplinary. Your research team is the colleagues you work with locally to conduct your research, and the colleagues and even industries globally who conduct similar research to you.

Refining your researcher identity includes thinking about your vision, your statement on how you believe your research will change society, and your unique approaches and methods that can make this happen. It is what you want to achieve in the long run. Your vision for the next five years is good for now. It's about tuning in to what drives you each day.

I'm not talking about your research title or status in terms of being a lecturer, senior lecturer, associate professor, professor or director. It's not that nobody cares – it's that many people do not understand what your title means. Taking more time to think about and refine your researcher identity matters because when you determine your researcher identity, you identify where you sit relative to your research team and competitors. Then you can see what you need to do to really stand out.

Researcher identity

Where are you positioned within the body of knowledge?

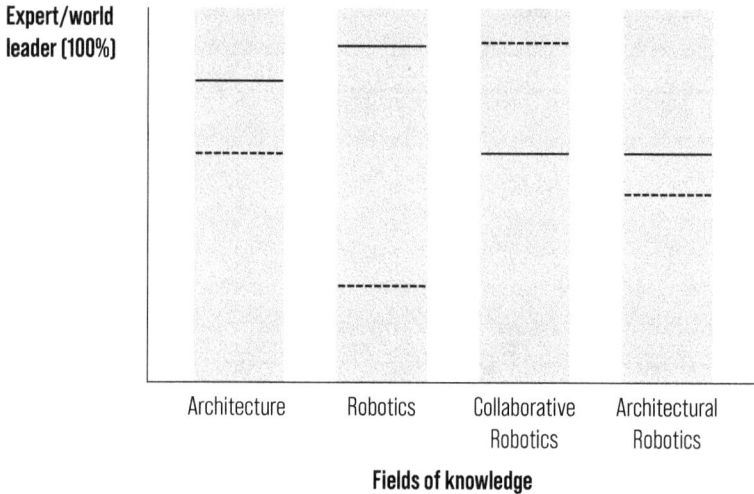

----- Your position ——— Other researchers' position

Source: Write Persuasively Toolkit, klgcommunications.com.au

Glenda worked up her researcher identity and really sharpened the way she presents her expertise, giving her confidence to define who she is as a researcher and where she is going with her research career. Let's see how determining her researcher identity worked for her.

Glenda identified her fields of knowledge as being architecture, robotics, collaborative robotics and architectural robotics. Her PhD was in architecture, and over time Glenda's expertise has evolved into the use of robotics in architecture, so she identifies her position in the architectural field as around 60%.

In the field of robotics, Glenda can confidently say her expertise is different from those researching the perception and localisation of robotics or how autonomous vehicles use robotics to track their location, for example. She identifies her position against other researchers in her team and competitors at 25%.

Glenda is focused on collaborative robotics – how a human and robot can work together to achieve a task. Here Glenda is leading the way. Her research examines how manufacturing tasks use a 'space systems' process, and she applies design principles into this architectural space. She positions her identity as being 90% compared with her colleagues and competitors.

Glenda identified she is an emerging leader in a fourth field, the architectural robotic field of knowledge with the vision to strongly incorporate her fundamental architectural knowledge into the robotic space. That is, to use industrial robotics on a large scale. It is a very new field and Glenda positions her identity here at 50%.

You don't have to be an expert in every field to be an expert in a research field that is a combination of knowledge areas. Together, all four fields enable Glenda to see her current identity, how each field relates to or builds on previous experience – or does not – and where she wants to go in the future to develop her expertise and vision to have an identity as a global leader in architectural robotics.

Consider her position of 60% in the field of architecture. Glenda knows her current identity, sees where she is compared with her colleagues and competitors, and has indicated she is comfortable in this position and sees no reason to push ahead in this field.

An identity at 25% in the field of robotics differentiates Glenda and her research approach. She is not concentrating on robotics and wants to push ahead in the fields of collaborative and architectural robotics.

An identity of 90% in collaborative robotics indicates there are a few global leaders either doing more or something different from her. Identifying these 'others' helps Glenda to reflect on:

- who these researchers are, where they are and what they are doing

- whether she needs to do something different with her research approach to have an identity as a global leader in this field. For example, could she invite these researchers to work with her on a new project and contact them to discuss, or invite them to attend a conference she is organising? Or simply examine what they are doing?

This snapshot of Glenda's identity is as a researcher, now and where she wants to be – her current identity, moving to her future identity. Glenda is really focused on moving up in this field of architectural robotics and has specific plans for the next five years to realise her vision.

This refinement step sharpens your understanding of why you need to be clear on your identity and value as a researcher. You might feel you don't want to compare yourself with your research team or your competitors, but doing so will make your researcher identity stronger and allow you to stand out more. The researcher identity diagram is an easy way to start this refining process.

Maryanne leads the Centre for Child and Family Studies. Each of the centre's team members recently undertook the researcher identity activity. This is important for the multi-disciplinary centre. Its members work at the intersection of health, education and community to 'positively transform the lives of children and families'. Maryanne wanted the members to be proud of their researcher identity, and to say it and write it succinctly.

You might think these exercises are challenging. Maryanne's team did. It was the two-part process that simplified how they wrote about their positions. Use your researcher identity diagram and notes to describe your vision and help you tune in to writing a strong and consistent researcher identity.

CREATING YOUR RESEARCHER IDENTITY STATEMENT

Now it's time to put all of your responses to the researcher identity questions in this chapter into one document. Name it, 'Researcher identity statement – first draft'. Leave the questions in as subheadings to guide you.

All researcher identity statements need a powerful opening statement. Have a look at these suggestions. Choose one of these sentence stems and try it as your opening statement.

- I am a leader in the field of X working at the intersection of a, b and c, serving to … (solve the problem X of the planet).

- I am a recognised leader in X, and the specific area of Y where I … (do amazing things).

- I am leading a transformation in …
- I am known/renowned internationally as/for/ …
- I trigger impactful outcomes by …
- I am at the forefront of … through my …
- As an X academic/researcher/scholar my career is hallmarked by Y and its successful application to …

Here are three examples:

> *I use human rights law to examine environmental problems, particularly those arising from climate change, to argue that governments are violating human rights by failing to protect the environment.*

> *I am an applied economist who uses econometric modelling to inform a range of socio-economic phenomena observed in Australia and internationally.*

> *I am a member of the Digital Media Research Centre, investigating the politics of social media platforms, particularly online discriminatory practices, hate speech and misinformation.*

Consider the three example sentences above and how they establish the identity of their researchers. When you play with your sentence, be sure your research, vision and what you have to say fit within your academic and/or industry profile and how you want to be perceived. First sentences make an immediate impact, and they begin the branding of who you are. Put the very best words in the very best order to position you and your research and research area. Grab your audience's attention immediately. Make them curious and want to read on.

It's okay if you feel challenged doing this. That's why you can't rush it. These two parts of thinking about and expanding your researcher identity take time. And your researcher identity is always changing.

Your identity changes as your unique life and professional experiences change. Your identity also changes as your expertise develops or becomes refined in a specific area, or you finalise a new methodology or method after a three-year project, or you win a grant.

We talked about Karin earlier. She is an emerging leader in paediatric pain, focusing on reducing pain and distress during children's medical treatment, specifically cancer care, and improving psychological health outcomes related to pain. Karin completed two long-term projects over the last year that added value to her expertise. This made her stand out so much she has recently received a grant valued at almost $500,000! She was also nominated as Chair of the Australian Pain Society's paediatric pain special interest group. She knew to update her researcher identity as these projects made her stand out from everyone in her field.

Review your researcher identity annually or when there have been significant changes. Use your Excel spreadsheet or PepTalkHer app where you have recorded your successes and achievements.

Make time to think about how you are positioned in your research field, where and why you belong in this field, and where you are positioned within your research team. Then make time to describe your vision and what drives you. Doing this step is critical for your success.

Now that you have a first draft of your researcher identity, you can join the elite club of people who have a great way of saying why they matter and what their researcher identity is. When you refine this draft, you will have a 500-word version when you need it for a conference presentation, for example. With a little more effort, you can refine it down to 300 words for publications or 100 words for your university website profile.

When participants in the Women in Research program do this exercise, they write even more succinctly to get a 75-word biography. When your identity is clear, it will be clear to others and clear in everything you write.

CONCLUSION

In this chapter, you have learned the killer move and part one of the persuasive writing process: making time to think. You learned the value of not rushing your writing. Dedicating time to the two parts of establishing your researcher identity will be time well spent, and will save you time later, all the way to the completion of your document.

When you allocate time to do this step of deep thinking, answering the researcher identity questions and using the researcher identity diagram, you will have your first draft of your researcher identity statement. Crafting these responses into a strong and succinct statement sets you up for personal and professional success. Ultimately, your ability to write persuasively will deliver more time into your career and opportunities will come your way.

Stop believing your researcher identity is already well understood. It probably isn't, especially outside your immediate circles. Start thinking what it would be like to have your researcher identity *singing*, where people say, 'Her social and intellectual commitment to this topic is unquestionable and her ability to translate the findings of her research is noteworthy and deserves commendation.' Imagine the funding that will come your way when this is how people see you! Make time in your life to establish your researcher identity, a step that will mark you out as a real professional in your field because so few people do it.

In the next chapter, I'm going to show you how dedicating yourself to specific reading projects by allocating time to read will elevate you again to the next level. It's not about glancing through magazines and journals. When people allocate time to read, they nail their writing in a way that sets them distinctly apart. Let's find out how.

✒ CHAPTER 4 ACTIVITIES

Allocate time to do some deep thinking – spend one hour every second day for two weeks. The alternate days give you time to reflect and let your ideas percolate in your brain. Or you might double this allocation, as thinking and writing the answers below does take time.

Prepare to write your researcher identity by answering these questions.

What makes you unique?

Here is an example of a unique point.

> *My years nursing chronic wounds enabled me to develop a risk assessment tool for delayed healing of chronic wounds which predicts with 80% accuracy whether a wound will heal within 24 weeks.*

Here is another example.

> *My real-world experience as a teacher and leader in remote schools means Resource X, which I developed, will build trauma-informed teachers who can support students and address trauma behaviours of children in remote communities.*

Here is an example of another unique point.

> *I examine through the lens of neuroscience the impact of complex trauma – physical, emotional and sexual abuse, serious neglect, and family violence – on brain development and functioning, and the school experiences of victims.*

Remember your unique point is not the same as your differentiator. Identifying what makes you unique and different from your colleagues is challenging. Your unique point can include personal attributes and experiences. Your differentiator could be the difference between your expertise and that of your colleagues in your field.

What is your differentiator?

Here is an example of a differentiator.

I research stakeholder and community engagement as a relational communication process that aims to build social capital and contribute to civic outcomes.

Here is another example.

I am an expert symmetric (not asymmetric) cryptologist investigating encryption algorithms that use shared secret keys to protect information.

What is it about your uniqueness and differentiator that makes you valuable?

Here is an example.

I am an interaction analyst whose research explores the hidden worlds of children's lives in the home, school and playground. I use video-ethnography and video-stimulated accounts to involve children as analysers of their own experiences, and teacher-researchers to reflect on their own practice. I work with the Department of Education to create professional learning resources for educators that identify effective communicative strategies between educators and children. My research develops empirically informed teaching strategies that help educators create safe and supportive social environments for learning.

Here is another example.

My unique factor is my national reputation in consumer partnership methods, enabling successful health and medical research that involves consumers. My differentiator (from other consumer behaviour researchers) is my accreditation in Luma design thinking, democratising knowledge that gives people a voice and allows them to be active participants in decision-making processes that affect their lives.

What examples tell your story?

I'm assuming you have a file for all your achievements. Perhaps you have an Excel spreadsheet on your desktop. You can use these examples to illustrate how you and your research are distinct. If you don't have a file, start one immediately!

I like the PepTalkHer app. You can use it to keep track of your career wins and the milestones you hit, and save emails from happy clients and photos of events where you present. This evidence builds your researcher identity. When you keep it up to date, it will surprise you how successful you have been. The PepTalkHer app is suitable for everyone to use.

Keep all the information from this exercise together because you will use it in a moment to craft a complete researcher identity statement.

*

All researcher identity statements need a powerful opening statement. Have a look at these suggestions. Choose one of these sentence stems and try it as your opening statement.

- I am a leader in the field of X working at the intersection of a, b and c, serving to … (solve the problem X of the planet).
- I am a recognised leader in X, and the specific area of Y where I … (do amazing things).
- I am leading a transformation in …

- I am known/renowned internationally as/for/ …

- I trigger impactful outcomes by …

- I am at the forefront of … through my …

- As an X academic/researcher/scholar my career is hallmarked by Y and its successful application to …

Here are three examples:

I use human rights law to examine environmental problems, particularly those arising from climate change, to argue that governments are violating human rights by failing to protect the environment.

I am an applied economist who uses econometric modelling to inform a range of socio-economic phenomena observed in Australia and internationally.

I am a member of the Digital Media Research Centre, investigating the politics of social media platforms, particularly online discriminatory practices, hate speech and misinformation.

CHAPTER 5

Step 2: Make time to read beyond the obvious

NAIL WHO WILL BENEFIT FROM YOUR RESEARCH

As a researcher, you already spend mountains of time reading. In this chapter, we are going to consider a different kind of reading. Dedicating yourself to specific reading projects, beyond the obvious, will elevate you to the next level. You must read to identify and understand who you are trying to influence, to gain deeper insights into your audiences. You will nail your writing when you allocate time to read the publications that matter to your readers, and you will begin influencing them in a way that sets you apart.

In this chapter, we're not talking about the reading you do to understand your topic or the reading you do for your literature review and to stay abreast of the latest developments in your research area. I want to shift the way you think about where you publish your research. If you want to influence other researchers in your field, you need to read to identify those researchers. These people are your target research influencers. Some of these will be people you already know. Some may have previously rejected your articles or grant submissions.

How many of the people in your field do you know? How many have heard of you?

If you want to influence the people who benefit from your research, you need to identify what these people read. Changing people's minds is difficult, and your research needs to be shared with many minds. Let's find out who your target research influencers are, including those outside your academic area. We want to get inside their heads, find out what they read and what they care about, and then target them. Make time to read about who will benefit from your research, and what your potential readers want to hear. You can then go about persuading them of the benefits of your work and ensuring your research translates into real-world impact.

Dedicating yourself and allocating time to such reading projects differs from the reading for your literature review. Try reading about potential stakeholders or industry partners or what your professional organisation has to say. For example, those of you in the engineering field are likely members of the national organisation Engineers Australia. Or perhaps you are an agronomist and you need to read about national or regional farming needs through the Department of Agriculture, Fisheries and Forestry. You might target an article about the economics of your research to a farming magazine, or farmers may even listen to the radio for the latest relevant economic news. You need to know this to reach your target audience.

Try reading beyond the obvious to identify the real people or groups whose lives will benefit from your research. It may not happen today or tomorrow, but this is the real reason you are a researcher – these people who read about your research, trust you and act on what you say. They are the influencers, the people who can get your research closer to those who need or will benefit from what you do.

Influencing your field happens one step at a time. It starts with reading popular articles, popular magazines and websites, the everyday news, mainstream newspapers, renowned magazines, *The Conversation*, LinkedIn and the professional magazines in your field. Going back to basics and thinking about the real problem you want to solve will help you identify who is most likely to help you achieve the impact you want. You have multiple audiences you need to influence. Identify the range of sources available in your field, and the minds of the people who read them. These are your target research influencers.

It might seem an unnecessary task to allocate time to a reading project other than for your literature review, but when you are making discoveries that can change the world, you need to remind yourself who you are researching for and who will spread your words the farthest.

Agricultural researcher Max allocated some time to reading about his target research influencers. Despite his topic, he had never thought about what farmers read or even what mattered to them most. He knew they wanted to intensify cereal production in the subtropical regions of Australia. Max didn't understand as much about how, or what was driving the need for intensification – whether it was the higher cost of fertiliser or greater competition from overseas. He did take time to identify the researchers who needed to hear about his work, and he did invite a senior manager from a peak agricultural industry organisation to his presentation.

This was a good move, but he hadn't thought all the way to the farmers in the field. At the end of his presentation, Max was asked how the farmers were going to get access to his critical strategies. They were the real people who needed to know how to better manage cereal production. Max then had to write another document for his *real* audience.

When you allocate time to identify who will read your research, who will believe you and who will act on what you say – like the farmers in the field – you will nail your writing in a way that sets you apart. You will influence your field one step at a time, and you can provide the right information in the right way to influence the right people. Remember, these people also influence each other, which means every step you take amplifies you and your research.

MAKE TIME TO IDENTIFY WHO NEEDS YOUR RESEARCH

In chapter 1, you discovered who needs your research. Now you're going to deepen your understanding of that group. Making time to identify who needs your research means identifying your target research influencers, your audiences, what they need to hear and why. It also means deepening your understanding of your audiences by reading what they read.

If you want to be successful, you need to know about your audiences. You need to read about what is driving them and identify their emotional needs. Think about those farmers. How is your research tied into their love of the land and their need to feel competent and to do a good job? What are the needs of the pharmaceutical companies who will produce your invention? Consider the cognitive needs of your audiences, their ability to understand your research and how they might learn, and even where they received their education.

Have you read about the physical and professional needs of your readers? Have you thought about the way you present your latest farming research? Does it facilitate the critical decisions farmers need to make about their soil testing, seed selection or livestock care? Or the pharmaceutical companies? Have you presented your technical data so they can translate it into clinical trials? What do the engineers who read *Create* need to know about deploying unmanned aerial vehicles to inspect the structure of bridges or survey telephone poles or cables in isolated areas?

Can you meet their professional needs to help them do their job competently? Where else can they go to get the latest research if you only publish in peer-reviewed journals? You need to tell them about your research in a manner in which they can receive it. This work all needs to be done before you start planning or writing. Ultimately, your audiences want to know about your work, and you can only give them this information once you have identified their emotional, cognitive, physical and professional needs.

This is not just about naming your audiences, like 'structural engineers in a large global engineering firm' or 'cattle farmers in Western Queensland', although this is important. Yes, you may be targeting structural engineers, but do they need to assess the Sydney Harbour Bridge accurately without stopping the 200,000 cars that cross it daily, and have workers suspended from ropes to identify the metal defects in the steel work connections? Or are they working on new train routes and need to understand how to cause minimal disruption to the local areas? And the farmers? They are under pressure to manage their greenhouse gas emissions and increase production to meet local and global demand. This is the level of detail you must understand. How can you write about your research so you persuade them to change the way they think and feel?

It might feel like this reading and preparation is overkill, but when your audiences know your message and understand your work is advancing knowledge and how this can benefit them, they will help you make an impact on society. If you want to be successful, you need to know what your audiences need, so you can tell them what they want to hear. Then you need to tell it clearly and simply. Try the KISS principle – Keep It Simple Scholar! Oh, I hear you laugh. You thought I was going to say Sweetheart! Or something else …

> This principle is so important, my colleague Asrul uses it every day. Asrul attended my workshops when he was a PhD candidate. Ten years later, as a supervisor and mentor of PhD candidates, he advocates strongly for the KISS principle when writing for multiple audiences and their multiple brains. You want them to receive your message.

> Consider Evonne's co-design project. Co-design researchers work with the people who need a problem solved. They use particular strategies to deepen their insights into what these people need.

> Evonne gave cameras to people living in aged-care homes to photograph the things they enjoyed doing each day. She also interviewed these people about what they enjoyed to more deeply understand the value of these activities. Drawing on the interview transcripts, the research team then created poems or poem-like prose from participants' words – see www.research.qut.edu.au/iacp/.

> These photographs and words were then displayed in multiple public exhibitions, including at the State Library of Queensland, to engage the public in a conversation about

the past, present and future of aged care. Together, these co-design and creative arts–based methods offered invaluable and memorable insights into what older people value in aged care. The profound understanding gained from this research has informed management and staff about methods to enhance the wellbeing of their residents, and challenged dominant sociocultural stereotypes that entering aged care is a fate worse than death. In reality, as the words and photographs vividly show, older people can live happily and healthily in aged care.

Never lose sight of who needs your research. Evonne understood the professional needs of the government departments and aged-care homes. Her audiences can trust what she says. Having co-designed her work with aged people, she understood the emotional, cognitive and physical needs of those in her research, giving them cameras to illustrate what makes them happy and an opportunity to tell their stories. She has nailed her writing, made an impact by telling the right people and providing the right information in the right way, and has distinguished herself as an impactful international leader in this area.

You may wonder why you need a deeper understanding of the cognitive, emotional and physical needs of those who will benefit from your research. Perhaps you have been more focused on the technical aspects of your research and not thought about the psychological or sociological needs. You may feel you lack the expertise or training in psychology or sociology to gain a deep understanding.

But there's no need to do an empirical study. It's about getting at least a feel for the cognitive, emotional and physical requirements of those who need and will benefit from your research. If you only think about your technical information, ask yourself what you want your readers to do with this information. In fact, it could be as easy as going into your professional organisation or talking with other people in your field.

Categorise your target research influencers and make sense of what they want or need to hear in this target research influencer table. Keep these details. You will need them in chapter 6 when you are planning what you write.

	Outside academia	Inside academia
Who are your target research influencers (audiences)? All the people who will benefit from your research.		
What do these influencers read?		
What do they want to hear? Why? What are their cognitive, emotional and physical needs? What is their agenda?		
What is the publishing medium?		
Where can you publish?		

Source: Write Persuasively Toolkit, klgcommunications.com.au

MAKE TIME TO ESTABLISH WHERE YOUR RESEARCH WILL BE MOST PERSUASIVE

The most reputable journals are where you should choose to tell the world about your work. Identify your research target audience by reading what they read.

Choosing what avenues best represent you and your research requires a good amount of reading time. There are two things to consider when choosing the journals where you will be most persuasive:

- Where is the more prestigious place for you to publish?
- Where will give you the greatest impact factors, like a Q1 journal in the top 25% of your subject area?

Identify the most-cited articles in these journals, the most credible and impactful, the top 1%. Add these journals to your target research influencer table above. You will need them in the following section. Check if each journal is going to help you reach the real audiences who will benefit most from your research.

I'm not talking about the usual reputable journals in your area. This is a mistake many researchers make. It's easier to outdo your competition if you publish more widely than the peer-reviewed journals everyone is publishing in. Think about reading extensively about your target research audience and use the information in your target research influencer table. You'll deepen your understanding of your target research influencers when you read what they read.

It might feel like this reading and preparation is time consuming. And it is – but the time you dedicate now to this level of reading will ensure you have the greatest and most extensive reach, and leave your competitors behind.

If you need proof of how you can leave your competitors behind by publishing outside of the usual peer-reviewed journals, think about Professor Brené Brown's TED Talk, 'The Power of Vulnerability', and Professor Adam Grant's book, *Give and Take*. Consider astrophysicist Neil deGrasse Tyson. He's a science communicator, has written popular science books and articles for *Scientific American*, *The New York Times* and many other outlets, and has presented on science-focused television programs.

How can you increase the visibility of your research to non-academic audiences? Think of the policymakers and public you will influence when you publish outside the usual journals. What about *The New York Times*, *Bulletin of the World Health Organization*, or you can even consider *The Wall Street Journal*, *Time* magazine and *The Guardian*. Where can you engage with audiences beyond academia?

You may think you and your research are not as prominent as Brown, Grant or Tyson. But you will be when you take the time to read and identify where to engage with your audiences beyond academia. Think about the most prominent people in your field. How are they influencing the people who benefit from their research?

Have a look where you have been publishing so far. Use your Google Scholar metrics or Scopus or other accepted measures to establish your greatest impact on science and your greatest impact on your field of research. Do these scores really establish the value of your research? How could you be more visible by publishing beyond academia?

There are also many places besides journals to publish – social media, the non-traditional research outputs (NTROs) used in creative industries, the ABC website, and many others. You started a list in your target research influencer table earlier. Keep adding to it.

Making the time to choose where your research will be most persuasive will set you up to influence more people. Remember, your responsibility as a researcher is to be read by as many people and as widely as possible.

MAKE TIME TO IDENTIFY HOW OTHERS HAVE REACHED AND INFLUENCED YOUR AUDIENCE

Now you have established the journal or other outlet that best meets your needs, make time to read three articles you find inspiring to use as models and to create a plan for writing your article. In chapter 7, I'm going to show you how to use these models to write your article.

Articles you find inspiring will encourage you to present research of a similar standard or better. These articles should make you feel positive and give you confidence about your research and your capacity to write something similar. An article can inspire you in terms of the way it is written, or the ideas and methods it presents.

The point of reading three articles is for you to use these as models for your own writing. When you use specific examples, you can understand what the journal expects. You can observe what a published writer has already done in creating that article. The model is a guide for when you write your article, instructing and illustrating how to write for that journal. Taking the time to read several articles and finding three you can use as models is an important part of the writing process. It'll save you a lot of time in writing and completing an article you are proud of, and it will make you feel comfortable about starting to write.

I'm not talking about choosing all excellent models. I want you to include an article that doesn't meet your expectations, guiding you in the process of what *not* to do. Take time to identify the structure of the article, the style of writing, and the way language is used. When writing coaches and educators talk about writing, they look at the way text is structured or organised, then the style of writing and how persuasive it is. The last thing they check is the grammar.

Maybe you have never taken the time to deconstruct an article in this manner, but learning to write persuasively is a skill, which means you can practise to get better. Most of the readers of your articles have PhDs and publish themselves, so they expect to read an article written in a particular way. Having a model will guide you. Reading articles where you want to publish and identifying articles you like will help you understand how others have already reached and influenced your audience. It's that simple.

You might already have your own model on which to base your writing, but using models from where you want to publish will save you time and mental energy. You do not have to reinvent the wheel. When you find a model that is inspiring, it will be because the article is easy to read, written with its audience in mind, and sells the benefit of the research.

Here's an activity for you. Download and print the three articles you are going to use as models. Make a note of what you like and dislike about them, and state why. Now have some fun. Pull out your highlighter pens. Choose three colours that have meaning for you. For example, mine are light blue, fluorescent green and orange.

Light blue, for me, means structure – the way the document is organised. It's the 'recipe' for articles, theses or TED Talks. There is even a recipe for abstracts and literature reviews. You need to follow the recipe so your readers can recognise what type of document you have written. You're going to read each of these articles twice. In the first read of each article, use your light-blue highlighter to identify all the headings and subheadings. These headings and subheadings serve as organisers. The order in which you present them guides your readers and therefore determines your success at persuading them. Check these headings against the journal guidelines. Note the words used. Are they the usual – introduction, methods, results – or do they guide you to differentiate this research and make it stand out and persuade? Look at the first heading – is it 'introduction'? What does this word tell you about this research? Nothing, except you're at the beginning. What is it an introduction to? Can you, as a writer, be more specific and give the reader a real clue, an immediate insight to your research? Can you persuade them right at the beginning that this is important research?

Now grab your second colour for a second read. Green means go, for me. Highlight all the phrases or expressions the author uses that show impact, that sound cool, that are used often or that you find interesting. You might use these in your own writing.

The third colour, orange for me, means warning. Highlight information you need to take notice of or want to think harder about later.

Keep your work from this exercise. You will transfer it to an exercise midway through chapter 6. There, you will create your own article recipe using the headings and subheadings from this model. And you will add all the style points to your template.

If you struggle to justify printing these articles because you are saving paper and the environment, keep in mind that printing your models means you can read them anywhere you choose in your designated reading time. And there is increasing evidence showing readers engage more with text on paper than on a screen. Making time to read will save you time later and will guide you in writing efficiently and effectively.

CONCLUSION

In this chapter, you have learned the value of dedicating time to reading so you can identify who benefits from your research and the cognitive, emotional and physical needs your research fulfils so you can influence your readers. It's a distinct kind of reading few researchers do, not to find out more about your topic but about those you need to persuade – your target research influencers.

Stop thinking you don't know who your audience is or what their needs are or what they read. And don't think you already know what your readers need. Start thinking about all the people who will benefit from your research and the range of publishing media where you will reach those who need to believe and act on your research.

Be sure to do your target research influencer table, categorise your research, categorise your target research influencers, and make sense of what they want or need to hear. And make time to identify how others have reached and influenced your audience. Now you know the value of the reading stage, which is step two of *The Five-Step Writing Framework*. These activities will elevate you to the next level, ahead of the competition.

In the next chapter, I will give you some tips for planning that winning document.

CHAPTER 5 ACTIVITIES

Categorise your target research influencers and make sense of what they want or need to hear in this target research influencer table. Keep these details. You will need them in chapter 6 when you are planning what you write.

	Outside academia	Inside academia
Who are your target research influencers (audiences)? All the people who will benefit from your research.		
What do these influencers read?		
What do they want to hear? Why? What are their cognitive, emotional and physical needs? What is their agenda?		
What is the publishing medium?		
Where can you publish?		

Source: Write Persuasively Toolkit, klgcommunications.com.au

*

Here's an activity for you. Download and print the three articles you are going to use as models. Make a note of what you like and dislike about them, and state why. Now have some fun. Pull out your highlighter pens. Choose three colours that have meaning for you. For example, mine are light blue, fluorescent green and orange.

Light blue, for me, means structure – the way the document is organised. It's the 'recipe' for articles, theses or TED Talks. There is even a recipe for abstracts and literature reviews. You need to follow the recipe so your readers can recognise what type of document you have written. You're going to read each of these articles twice. In the first read of each article, use your light-blue highlighter to identify all the headings and subheadings. These headings and subheadings serve as organisers. The order in which you present them guides your readers and therefore determines your success at persuading them. Check these headings against the journal guidelines. Note the words used. Are they the usual – introduction, methods, results – or do they guide you to differentiate this research and make it stand out and persuade? Look at the first heading – is it 'introduction'? What does this word tell you about this research? Nothing, except you're at the beginning. What is it an introduction to? Can you, as a writer, be more specific and give the reader a real clue, an immediate insight to your research? Can you persuade them right at the beginning that this is important research?

Now grab your second colour for a second read. Green means go, for me. Highlight all the phrases or expressions the author uses that show impact, that sound cool, that are used often or that you find interesting. You might use these in your own writing.

The third colour, orange for me, means warning. Highlight information you need to take notice of or want to think harder about later.

Keep your work from this exercise. You will transfer it to an exercise midway through chapter 6. There, you will create your own article recipe using the headings and subheadings from this model. And you will add all the style points to your template.

CHAPTER 6

Step 3: Make time to plan in two steps

REVOLUTIONISE YOUR PURPOSE AND YOUR DOT-POINT PLAN

So you have been told to plan your writing. This chapter presents a revolutionary two-step planning process:

1. The purpose statement.
2. The rock-solid dot-point plan.

You've may have tried to write a dot-point plan and had little or no success because you missed the first step, the purpose statement. The purpose statement builds on the work of the previous chapters. We're going to look at everything that's unique about you and your research, then use this logical two-step process that totally changes the planning game.

Planning using a two-step process is fundamental to your success as a published researcher. Step one is your purpose statement, the argument you will present in your document. Step two is your plan, a dot-point outline of the document you are going to write. It is all the ideas you want to write in this document, which you then prioritise. This two-step plan will save you time and mental and physical energy.

It's not about rushing your purpose statement or doing a quick outline. I'm talking about taking the time to plan your purpose statement – an explicit statement that is based on an argument or problem and tells your readers what your article is about. It is the foundation of everything you write, guides the examples you choose and presents an answer to your argument.

Step two will be a detailed plan that includes all the headings and subheadings of your article, established in chapter 5 as the structure. It is the plan of all your ideas written as dot points, guided by your purpose statement.

It might feel like doing this level of planning is restrictive and will stifle your creativity. Or maybe you're thinking that if you're already writing a detailed plan, why not just write the whole thing? But you must be able to organise your ideas well to argue that your approach is the most effective way to investigate your research problem, that your outcome is significant, and to see the structure of your argument. You must do this if you want to be successful.

You've already defined the value of your research in chapter 1, and you've made time to think in a way that no-one you are competing with thinks. Then, in chapter 5, you made time to read – and not the way everyone else reads. You're going to use these new skills to craft your purpose statement, which will launch you and your research into the world. Time to plan the right way means your planning will work and save time, not like the plans of the past.

I like the way Meggie Palmer from PepTalkHer describes ditching the New Year's resolution and making a plan.* She wrote:

> I've lived in New York for more than five years. But I still find myself getting lost – a lot.
>
> Geography isn't my strong point. Plus there's always something to distract me – a new bar that's popped up, a boutique that looks interesting to pop my head into, or a statue I've never noticed before.
>
> If I don't plug my destination into my phone and map the best route? I'll inevitably get lost.

She clearly has a sense of purpose – her destination. When she doesn't set out with a purpose statement, she gets distracted. She wanders around New York, where there is always something to distract her. It is the purpose statement that makes the plan work.

In this chapter, I'll show you how to wrap up everything you've done in this book so far into a powerful purpose statement. You'll use it to make a dot-point plan as detailed as a roadmap of New York.

Planning the purpose for your writing, and then what it is you are going to write, demands your time. This first step will take you about one hour to develop.

MAKE TIME TO WRITE YOUR PURPOSE STATEMENT

Here you are, and it's time to write your purpose statement. Let's start with Angie and Mark's purpose statement story.

Angie phoned me late one Friday afternoon. She had been writing an article with her more senior colleague Mark and

---

* www.peptalkher.com/blog/a-simple-career-plan-works.

felt they were going nowhere. There was no story, and they couldn't agree on the focus. The article had to be submitted by Sunday evening. Angie had been in one of my workshops and knew about the purpose statement. She had tried to demonstrate and convince Mark but struggled to make headway.

I invited them both to my office and we set about writing the purpose statement. We had some unpacking to do with the article Angie and Mark were working on, and by 7:00 pm we had completed both step one – the purpose statement – and step two – the dot points for their article. When they left, they were comfortable knowing what to do to write a fabulous article and meet the Sunday deadline – and they did.

Every researcher needs to explicitly state the purpose of their article. With researchers increasingly writing articles with a series of co-authors, this step can be difficult and time consuming, to-ing and fro-ing between you.

How do you agree on what your article is about? Make it easy. Use step one and write a purpose statement together. Do it at the beginning. That explicit statement based on an argument or problem tells your readers what your article is about. I use the word 'article', but this is relevant for every type of document you write. Proposals, presentations and keynote speeches are all examples of where you are persuading your readers, your listeners and your audiences to change the way they think or to act in a new manner.

Your purpose statement should be *one sentence only*. It captures what your research is all about. It is an explicit statement based on an argument or problem, succinctly telling your readers what your article is about. It's the foundation for everything you write and it guides the examples you choose to persuade your readers. Your purpose statement presents a possible answer for your argument or research problem. It also serves to persuade your readers, motivate them with your new ideas and inspire them because you have found a solution to a particular problem.

I'm not talking about writing numerous sentences in your purpose statement using terms of deficit like 'research gap', or writing about what you were aiming to do when you started your work. I'm talking about taking one hour to write one sentence. About an hour works when you follow the recipe. Following the recipe means you will present your new idea, the outcome of your research and what you are selling about your outcome. The focus of your statement will then be positive, and the focus is the subject of your research.

You might feel you cannot put your entire research project into one sentence and that writing one sentence shouldn't take an hour. But in my 20-plus years' experience working with researchers, this is exactly the process. Writing your purpose statement moves you from reporting or informing your audiences about what you did during your research project to arguing why your research is so fantastic. When you create a specific purpose statement for every document you write, you'll be writing words that influence.

Taking one hour now to plan and write your purpose statement means you will know what you are writing about and ensure you are writing to persuade your readers. Have a look at this example of a purpose statement. You will write several versions to get it right during your hour. The example below shows the evolution through three of the eight attempts of a purpose statement model.

Draft 1

That older people living with HIV can receive the healthcare they need, at the time they need it when <u>peer workers and clinicians work collaboratively at the top of their scope</u>.

Feedback: the underlined section needs defining.

Draft 2

That the Researcher's super plan will enable/guide peer workers and clinicians to work collaboratively and provide the healthcare older people living with HIV need, and in a timely manner.

Draft 3

That the Researcher's super co-designed model of care will enable peer workers and clinicians to work collaboratively (at their optimal scope) and ensure people living with HIV have access to safe, responsive and inclusive healthcare.

You will know when your purpose statement is right. You will feel it is right. Plus, you can test it. Say it aloud and ask your colleagues if they completely understand your argument. If they don't, let them ask you questions. Your responses will make you refine and clearly state your purpose.

When you make time to plan what it is you are arguing, you establish and put words to the most critical idea. It will be the key outcome or new thing about your research that you are selling for this document. Doing so will save you time, and let you write strongly and start establishing your research expertise. You can sell your entire project before anyone even reads your article.

You might be thinking, *I can't decide what I should sell here. I have so much information from my research.* If you can't decide what you are arguing, how will your readers understand what you have achieved? How can they understand your research if you don't articulate it? It's expecting too much of people. What will they think of you as a researcher?

Try this easy strategy to write a fabulously strong and clear purpose statement. Thousands have done it successfully and are doing it today. Join the club.

Persuasive writing is effective writing. It is clear, accurate and concise. Your audience must be able to quickly, effortlessly and unambiguously understand what you say. You'll know when your purpose statement is right. You have that a-ha! moment of clarity.

Your turn to write your purpose statement. Start with this sentence stem:

The purpose of writing this document is to persuade my audiences that …

Be sure to keep this sentence opening exactly as it is. Leave in the word 'that'.

To complete this sentence, think about your outcome. What about your research is so important? Who is going to benefit from your work? Why do your readers need to care?

Keep in mind these tips for writing a purpose statement:

- Start by placing each idea on a new line.
- Make sure the focus is on the subject of your research. For example, the first word after 'that' should be the subject of your research, the key information, the thing you are selling and arguing is super-duper. It can be the outcome of your research, or in some statements the purpose may be to sell the new method you established.
- Keep the focus positive.
- Be sure you present a new idea.

Look at the examples here of good purpose statements. They are not perfect, but are models to get you started.

The purpose of this document is to persuade my readers *that* ...

- ☑ ... re-engaging older workers into paid employment by just 5% will boost the economy by $48 billion each year.

- ☑ ... students' spatial experience in urban vertical schools is critical to establish how these school typologies impact student wellbeing.

- ☑ ... model X using ICP-MS* and chemometrics combined will identify heavy metal content in Brisbane water at times of changing climatic conditions such as drought and flood.

- ☑ ... the KNW framework* will normalise therapeutic hospital landscape design and significantly contribute to positive health outcomes for hospital patients, their families, staff and administrators.

- ☑ ... Sadia's online Questionnaire Design Model* enables the voice of an underrepresented group – women – to be heard in a patriarchal society, creating a more inclusive built environment.

Obtain feedback from your colleagues. They don't have to know or be familiar with your research. They will ask you questions if your statement isn't clear. This valuable information, gained before you start writing, will set you on a clearer writing journey.

Make sure your one sentence is not more than 25 words. Put your purpose statement in the header of your document. When you see it

---

* Create a brand name that establishes your researcher identity and enables others to reference your research output.

all the time, you will be reminded to stay on track and only include information that sells your research.

I love this strategy. I see the benefits every day with writers who now argue that their research will change the planet.

You might struggle to do this exercise or say it's hard to be that concise, or that you're still unsure what your purpose is, that you've never thought about your research in this way or that you're not good at arguing. But writing your purpose statement is the step that changes your work into a persuasive document. It's the step that makes plans come to life and makes them purposeful. Writing a purpose statement is the missing element for many writers. When you've written it well, you will know it's right. It reflects exactly what you are doing. It is the reason you have to articulate what you want to achieve before you start. It's much easier to do this before you put pen to paper.

MAKE TIME FOR A DOT-POINT PLAN BEFORE YOU WRITE

Making time to plan before writing was a skill I learned in my undergraduate days. Exams were three hours long. We had to write three essays of 800 to 1000 words each, and then two plans so detailed that someone else could write the essay from them. This strategy was so powerful, I've never forgotten it. I use it every single day, and I teach it.

Now you are at step two: you are going to create your dot-point plan. Start by writing your clearly established purpose statement in the header of your page. Step one, the purpose statement, is the defining difference of your work. Placing it in the header means you see it on every page. And it is going to guide your destination in the crowded streets of New York, all before you start writing in sentences.

The dot points are your concise ideas listed as if they are mini-headlines, with a series of ideas under a heading or subheading and not written in full sentences. Just like in the example here.

The purpose of this book is to argue that persuasive writing means engaging in *The Five-Step Writing Framework* – taking time to think, read, plan, write, revise – if you want to be successful.

Things to remember about writing persuasively:

- takes time
- is an iterative process
- has steps:
  - think:
    - about yourself as a writer of research
    - define your researcher identity
    - know your differentiator
    - what makes you unique
  - read:
    - about your target research influencers
    - establish where your research will be most persuasive
    - identify models to guide your writing
  - plan:
    - purpose statement
    - dot-point plan
  - write:
    - annual writing plan (six steps)
    - know the recipe
    - make research terms consistent
    - align research question, aims, objectives
    - write about impact

- first draft (four steps)
  - revise:
    - feedback
    - edit
- should aid thinking
- guides you to:
  - refine
  - reshape

  your purpose and argument
- needs you to give yourself permission to carry out the process and evolve
- your aim is to:
  - present and highlight the contribution of your:
    - research
    - researcher identity
    - vision
- have as many people as possible:
  - understand
  - be influenced by your research

I'm not talking about quickly using dot points just for some sections of your paper, I'm talking about the entire first draft of your document. This first draft needs to be all dot points, with your purpose statement written in the header of each page. It might feel like a lot of work. It is. It is detailed, and you are planning what you are going to write, breaking down your ideas into smaller chunks and showing how they are all related to each other.

You're going to have a very new experience of writing a dot-point plan now that you have a purpose statement. It is not *easy*, but it is easier. It keeps you focused on the destination. It's a plan to organise your ideas so that each idea adds weight to your argument. You can get great feedback at this stage of building your ideas. It's not as easy to get meaningful feedback when you write in long sentences.

> Consider Desi. She was nearing the completion of her thesis when she learned about the value of establishing a detailed plan using dot points. Frustrated with her efforts to get the feedback she needed, Desi tried the strategy. She presented a two-page dot-point plan – and voila! She was overwhelmed with the difference – the feedback was about her ideas and the flow of these ideas in that section of her thesis. Her dot points had been cross-checked with her argument, and the feedback showed this. Desi later said: 'The dot-point plan is a really meaningful and helpful strategy. Before knowing about this method, I felt lost in the jungle, overwhelmed with the data.' Desi has now expanded her dot points into paragraphs for her results chapter and eagerly awaits more feedback.

Desi is an example of how the dot-point plan works when combined with the purpose statement. It is a two-step process. Try the dot-point plan and organise your dot points. Are all your ideas there? Are they in the best order? Do they add weight to your argument? Obtaining feedback on your ideas at this stage will save you time and angst later while providing rich and meaningful information now, and it's also easier to make changes to your dot-point plan than it is to a complete draft.

You now know the dot-point plan is a powerful step in writing efficiently and successfully, if you use it with the purpose statement. I know it can be hard to try something new. It's often uncomfortable at the beginning and may take a while to get used to. In this chapter I have made it easier for you to get ready for your next article.

You might be thinking, *I've tried planning and I still get confused when I write*, or *I've tried planning and I end up writing it out in full*. To avoid these issues, get feedback on your plan while it's still in dot-point form. Ask for the right sort of feedback. Is your plan so thorough that your colleague could write it into a full article?

CONCLUSION

Now you have an approach to planning that will succeed every single time. It is a two-step process.

Step one is to draft a purpose statement for every document you write. Writing your one-sentence purpose statement will help you to influence your readers in every article you write.

Step two, the dot-point plan, is a different experience when you use it with the purpose statement clearly established and written in the header of your page.

You might feel uncomfortable about planning, feeling it takes longer because you need to break down your ideas into smaller chunks that are related to each other. You might be unsure at this stage about how to make all your points fit together in the overall plan. But now you can use this two-step process. Write your purpose statement, and get feedback on it. Plan your dot points and get feedback on them. Feel the power of knowing what you are writing before you start. Stop jumping straight into writing your article. Give your research a go.

Now you know how to get to your destination. In the next chapter, I will show you the steps that make writing a document as easy as a walk in the park.

Writing! What a breeze!

CHAPTER 6 ACTIVITIES

Try this easy strategy to write a fabulously strong and clear purpose statement. Thousands have done it successfully and are doing it today. Join the club.

Persuasive writing is effective writing. It is clear, accurate and concise. Your audience must be able to quickly, effortlessly and unambiguously understand what you say. You'll know when your purpose statement is right. You have that a-ha! moment of clarity.

Your turn to write your purpose statement. Start with this sentence stem:

> *The purpose of writing this document is to persuade my audiences that ...*

Be sure to keep this sentence opening exactly as it is. Leave in the word 'that'.

To complete this sentence, think about your outcome. What about your research is so important? Who is going to benefit from your work? Why do your readers need to care?

CHAPTER 7

Step 4: Make time to write efficiently and successfully

PERSONALISE YOUR ANNUAL WRITING PLAN AND COLLATE YOUR RECIPES

Of all the five steps in the writing process, this is the time you spend actually writing rather than thinking, reading and planning. Making time to write means deciding well ahead of time when in the year and when in the day you are going to write. All good writing follows a recipe.

We are going to keep it simple and use the word 'recipe' to define the particular structure where the writer has steps and tasks to follow to communicate and meet the expectations of the reader. Technically speaking, the term is 'genre', but I want you to know the recipe for every type of writing you do. Think of Nigella Lawson. If you want your chocolate cake to look and taste like Nigella's, you must follow her recipe. With my approach, you have an even better recipe because you have already taken the time to think, read and plan.

Let's look first at creating an annual writing plan. I'm going to describe later how to personalise it. In my world, this step means developing your annual writing plan by writing down when in the year you have deadlines for writing. You need to see all the writing you need to do for the year – the journal publications, keynote presentations, grant applications, promotion due dates – everything.

Then you need to know when in the day you write most effectively. Acknowledge that writing is a crucial part of your daily process. I'm not talking about cramming, I'm talking about knowing how much time you have in your year to write well so that every document you write is your best writing, that sells you and how fantastic your research is.

Knowing all of your writing responsibilities at the beginning of every year means you can be in control, and when more writing opportunities arise during the year you will know whether you can fit them in. Imagine you deliver the most brilliant presentation because you followed all the recipes and strategies in this book, and tell the world expert in your field that yes, you would love to write an article with them. And on looking at your annual writing plan, you can state exactly when you would be available.

It might seem like you are flat out researching, that it's excessive to be this organised, or there might be writing you must do that you're not yet aware of. But researchers never allow enough time to write, so writing down all your commitments for the year will show you how much you have to write. It will make you take your writing commitments seriously. You will see what type of writing is due when and what recipes you might need to use, and you will be mindful that writing is a process that takes time. Personalising your annual writing plan following the recipe in this book means you will get your writing done.

> We all know how competitive it is in academia. One of my researchers, Rowena, was advised to increase her publications one year. We filled out her annual writing plan and personalised it – writing down all of her writing commitments, her schedule and even the dates for when her dot-point plans were to be expanded to first drafts. She took her annual writing plan to her performance review meeting and could discuss each of her commitments, which of them were more valuable, and how she would go about achieving her targets and increasing her publication rate. Her supervisor was so impressed with her personalised plan, she said yes to funding Rowena's work with a writing coach – me. When you see what you have to do, you can make time to write efficiently, successfully and brilliantly.

This book is about the distinction between writing for research and writing for persuasion. This chapter is about the time you actually spend in the writing process and it starts with your annual writing plan. I'll start by detailing the plan and then look at how to personalise it. I'll give you the key recipe and a link to many other recipes which are all about being efficient and successful. Then, we will explore officially putting your words on the page to make an impact.

YOUR ANNUAL WRITING PLAN

Your annual writing plan must be personalised to be useful. Personalising your plan means deciding well ahead of time when in the year and also when in the day you write best. Keep your annual writing plan up to date and put the time in your calendar to write each day. When do you write best? When are you most effective? Are you a night owl or an early bird? Your body clock will tell you when you are most productive. Is it first thing in the morning before your family responsibilities, or later at night after them? We are all different.

> One researcher I work with has established an effective routine. She walks the dog, returns for a shower, then sits down to write for 90 minutes each day. She says she's alive from the walk and fresh from the shower. Then she rewards her excellent writing practice with a coffee before she heads into the office.

I'm not suggesting the morning or this particular strategy will work for you. Perhaps you are like Jane, in chapter 2, who books all day Friday in her calendar for writing at the State Library. That could work for you. It does not matter when or where it is – as long as you know when you will write and where you will write. It might seem out of the ordinary to think this deeply about your writing habits and strategies, but you will not stick to the plan if you don't make it personal. When you see how much writing you need to do for the year, you will recognise that allocating time every day, when you are most effective, will see you kicking goals.

> I created my annual writing plan, and by sticking to it I wrote this book in 90 days – 8:30 to 10:30 every morning, every day. The annual writing plan does more than list your writing commitments for the year. It sets you up to make time to write and begin the process of taking your writing seriously. If you are not sure when you work best, experiment. Is your brain at its best from 3:00 pm to 5:00 pm? Or when the sun comes up?

Here are the six steps of creating an annual writing plan:

1. Take time to list all your writing commitments for the year, including speeches, articles, media publications and LinkedIn.

2. Identify the journals where your research should be submitted. Consider if you have a good cross-section of journals. Is the list extensive or too narrow? Will you have as many people as possible read your research? Have you considered the special editions for this year? Transdisciplinary research warrants your careful attention.

3. Use your annual writing plan to make writing decisions. Is the plan realistic? Or do you need to cull? Will it guide you to say no when someone asks you to do more writing this year?

4. Create a list of reviewers, those who need to know about you and your research. Allocating people and having a timeframe for when you get feedback will ensure you are not rushing.

5. Use the dates in the plan to ensure you stay on track and meet your deadlines, and you are not rushing.

6. You can now craft your purpose statements for each of your writing commitments. They may change, but if you do these all at once you can make sure that every publication sells a different aspect of your work, and that you extend your research and your researcher identity as widely as possible.

Now schedule in your personal daily writing time. Think too about where you will write. Make it safe, conducive to writing and comfortable.

On the next page is the writing plan I use myself, and with my clients. You can download this from klgcommunications.com.au.

Annual Writing Plan
Publication and Presentation Details

Items/tasks	Journal name Due date for submission	Date for review	Reviewer name	Date for review comments	Date to incorporate feedback and action

Source: Write Persuasively Toolkit, klgcommunications.com.au

You might struggle to do this exercise because it seems overwhelming. You might think, *when I look at everything I have to write, I don't even want to start.* If so, maybe your personalised annual writing plan is telling you to cull some of your tasks. Work with a colleague to decide what you need to remove.

THE ABSTRACT – THE FUNDAMENTAL RECIPE FOR RESEARCHERS

Every form of writing requires a genre and an accepted and understood way of how a document should be composed. A genre is a shared set of communicative purposes, according to linguist and genre guru John Swales.

We agreed earlier to keep it simple and use the word 'recipe' instead of 'genre', to define the particular structure where the writer has steps and tasks to follow to communicate and meet the expectations of the reader. The most fundamental recipe for researchers is the abstract. Almost every type of writing is based on the abstract, especially the article, though there will be variations or extensions.

The work you did in the previous chapter – looking at the structure of existing articles in the publications you are targeting – was, in fact, discerning the recipe. This chapter is about defining the process of what you did, identifying the genre and looking at the recipe that's used in that genre. I have dozens of recipes for researchers, and as soon as a writer understands the recipe and why each part goes where, their writing becomes easier. These recipes include how to write: a literature review; discussion section; introduction to methods section; an entire thesis – monograph or by publication; results versus discussion; a promotion and grant proposal first sentence; and a keynote presentation.

I'm not talking about blindly following a list of tasks in a recipe. I'm asking you to fully understand why you start with A, finish with Z, and how the recipe allows the reader to follow and be influenced by your writing. You might feel you know these recipes or the order of writing tasks for your documents – you have been reading articles for years and most likely these aspects are intrinsic to you. I want you to make these recipes explicit. If you are going to persuade and influence your readers, you need to know the purpose of your writing.

Getting the genre right is a quick win. Getting it wrong is a quick loss. If you don't write according to the expected recipe of the genre, it doesn't matter about all the thinking you did or how brilliant your content is.

> Janice and Chaturanga have written winning grant documents, receiving thousands of dollars of funding. They found this success when they understood they were not writing one recipe – a report – but writing another – a proposal. They stopped describing their projects, and began persuading their assessors their fabulous approach and solution to a global research problem was unique and doable. Janice and Chaturanga are planning people. They had their plan and their recipe. Their funding success was based on understanding and working the recipe for a successful grant – the recipe to persuade and influence the reader.

You might think there are no recipes for writing, or you may wonder about your authenticity or how original you will appear if everyone follows the same recipe. All writing has structure, from a congratulatory note to a presidential speech. Knowing the structure for your type of writing and developing the right parts of it will enable your readers to follow along with you as you unfold your ideas to persuade them. You can't do that if you don't know the recipe.

Often, it's only writing coaches, editors or full-time writers who talk about the structure and use these terms, but the workshops I've been running for years teach researchers the recipes for every part of their writing. When you know these, you will make your writing process much more efficient.

Let's unpack the recipe for an abstract. Have a look at your latest abstract and see how closely it follows the recipe. Does it start with the **background** to your research problem, where you establish the criticality of your research? Have you followed this background detail with your **research problem**? When you have a problem, you **aim** to solve it, so have you written your aim next?

Objectives are how you achieve your aims. You only have three to five. Whether you include your objectives depends on how long your abstract is. Your readers want to know your particular **method** for solving your problem. They expect to read about your **results** or the **outcome** of your research. Ultimately, they want to know the **significance** of your research, of solving a problem of the planet, of the new knowledge you have created or what it means to your research fields. Can you recite this recipe in your sleep or tell a new researcher to your team the logical flow of this structure – the recipe for an abstract?

You might be thinking, *the recipe I use in my field is different.* If you know the difference, that's fantastic. If you don't, use the recipe above. All structures can be adjusted for particular purposes. Knowing the basics is key, and adjusting for your purpose will more effectively communicate your research.

BEFORE YOU PUT PEN TO PAPER - TWO KEY STRATEGIES

Make your work easier to write and easier for your readers to follow with these two strategies:

- Make your research terms consistent.

- Be ready to write about impact.

I'm going to explain what these strategies mean, and then you will try two exercises which will make it easier for you to create your first draft.

Using consistent terms

Writing clearly and using terms consistently gives your readers immediate access to your ideas. You can do this from the beginning before you even write. You can achieve a high readability factor when you align your research question with your research aim. If you have one research question, aim to solve that one question with one aim. Two questions, two aims.

Each aim has three to five objectives or actions to achieve this aim. When you complete your action, there will be an outcome. Stating the outcomes of each objective means you'll have three to five outcomes. Writing clearly about the significance of each of your three to five outcomes will establish the significance of your research.

You may think you automatically align your research terms and write about them consistently, but I developed this activity after seeing so many researchers not getting it right or using terms interchangeably and confusing their readers. You will practise this aligning activity in a moment. Make time before you put pen to paper and get it right. You will write effectively when you write consistently.

> Marianella's research is advancing the Australian medical technology (MedTech) sector, creating health-tech devices that are wearable and usable for people at home. Last year she was invited to resubmit a document based on the urgent need for her research. The first thing we did after refining her purpose statement was to align her research questions, aim, objectives, outcomes and significant statements. She used the strategy I have given you here.

> Having these terms clear and consistent meant that all of her writing became more readable and more accessible for her assessors. Marianella said her final submission was 1,000% clearer and more powerful. We hope her assessors agree.

Writing about impact

Most researchers don't think enough about the impact of their research. They are busy *doing* their research and then rushing to write about it to meet a deadline. I want you to be ready to write and to show your best. This strategy helps you tell others about the impact of your research and how it's significant to those for whom it matters. Start talking about what your research actually does and the benefits of it, rather than reporting or describing the details of what you do.

If you're going to earn the research dollar, people need to easily read your document and follow your ideas. They can do this when you present and refer to these ideas consistently. The assessors then want to know how your research is going to impact people socially, culturally or technologically, or to advance knowledge.

Consider this response Felipe received from a grant assessor:

'This project could indeed enable a range of business opportunities in Australia as the development of (X) can be done on existing drones to add value and create a niche market for Australia. This is a short- to medium-term benefit. I also see this project as a significant long-term benefit in expanding the operational domain of flying robots.'

This is the type of response Felipe was seeking. It is the type of response you are after – an assessor confirming that your method will have impact, in this case in the short, medium and long term in Australia, and impact the development of all flying robots.

Aligning your research question, aims and objectives with your outcomes means you will consistently guide your reader through your document all the way to your clearly thought out impact. Thinking about impact and writing in the exercise below means you will sell the benefit of your research all the way through your document. You will persuade your readers of the significance of your research – that your research matters.

You might think, *how can I use consistent terms and write about impact before I start writing?* Try these two activities and see how you go. I guarantee doing these before you start writing will make everything easier for you to write and clearer for your reader.

Activity 1

This is the 'magic table' I referred to in chapter 1. Now it's your turn to write persuasively by aligning your research question with your aim, objectives, outcomes and the significance of these outcomes.

Aligning your – research question + aim + objectives
+ outcome + significance

Research question	Aim	Objectives	Outcome/ deliverable	Significance
RQ 1	This research aims to 1. develop ...	This research will be achieved by (doing what?) i. identifying ...	1i	1i
		ii. evaluating ...	1ii	1ii
		iii. developing ...	1iii	1iii

Source: Write Persuasively Toolkit, klgcommunications.com.au

You can download this from klgcommunications.com.au.

Activity 2

Start talking about what your research *does* – the benefits of it – rather than describing the details of what you *do* by completing these sentences.

- This project will significantly impact ...
- This groundbreaking work ...
- This project will create local, national and international impact through ...
- This discovery of creating ... has ...
- The benefit of my research leads to ...

Keep your responses and file them in a folder called 'Why my research matters'.

If you have already started writing, you may be struggling to align your research terms, sort your ideas and be consistent. If so, stop what you are writing and work on completing these two key strategies. You will be amazed by how much easier it is to write – and write clearly – when you use consistent terms. And when you have three to five outcomes for each research question, you will be able to write about impact.

BRINGING EVERYTHING TOGETHER TO CREATE THE FIRST DRAFT

You are now ready to bring it all together into the first draft.

> Elaine's research is in hospital-associated infections, a seemingly dry area. By deconstructing the writing process and following the steps you're reading about now, Elaine told me she moved her writing up to another level altogether, achieving authoritative, beautiful and clear writing. That's where I want you to be.

At the stage of bringing everything together, putting pen to paper or fingers to the keyboard, think about all the preparation you have done. You have your purpose statement and dot-point plan for writing an article from chapter 6, with all your headings and subheadings. All the work you have done to this point has been to get you ready to write your first draft.

You might feel that after all of this thinking, reading and planning, you can write well immediately and make this draft your first *and* final draft. I can assure you this is not the case, especially if you are following my advice. You still have the revising stage to go. You will not be sitting down in one go to write your 5,000-word or 10,000-word article, funding proposal or promotion document.

Focusing on getting all the words down on the page takes time. Think about the scientists in the Centre for Agriculture where Peter has established a successful protocol with his research team. They would never think to write in one go. They are often moving from the desk out into the field for days to collect data on vegetation, soil and greenhouse gas samples. When back at the desk to write, they can be quickly interrupted to go and work in the lab. Peter expects his team to have their article recipe so well established they can easily identify where they are up to each time they return to the desk.

Such a practice is admirable. Daniel, one of Peter's former scientists, agrees, and attributes his success now as an Agricultural Soil Scientist at the European Commission to this great writing practice.

When you bring it all together and have your article recipe detailed, it's easy to leave your desk for any amount of time – going out into the field or into the laboratory – and know exactly what you are writing when you return.

You might think you can put all your words down, have the best words in the best order, and have your first draft as your only draft. But not even the best writers expect to be able to do this. JK Rowling rewrote the opening chapter of her first book a total of 15 times, having planned all the events of the series of seven books before she started writing the first.[*]

In her book *Overnight Authority* journalist and book coach Kath Walters advises writers to keep the reader receptive to our ideas – we want them to be 'in the zone', effortlessly connecting with what we say and gliding from one idea to the next without a hitch. This is

---

[*] www.nownovel.com/blog/five-great-writing-tips-from-j-k-rowling/.

the responsibility of the writer. You can effortlessly lead your readers through your document when you use consistent terms, align your research question, your aims and your objectives, and have your recipe with detailed dot points, ready for your first draft.

Try this four-step process:

1. Put your purpose statement in the header of your Word document. It will then be on every page and remind you that every time you write a word and expand a dot point, it needs to add weight to your argument.
2. Leave in all your headings and subheadings. They will guide you in expanding your dot points into full sentences.
3. Define and explain the points you have made. Give evidence and examples to support your argument.
4. Be sure to write in sections, one at a time, just like the example of the scientists in the Centre for Agriculture. Stick to the process – it works. Your ideas and facts are important. Get them written down in this first draft.

You may feel uncomfortable about your ideas sounding too simple or unsophisticated because you are turning dot points into sentences, or the flow is not right. Before you go about polishing this draft, you would benefit from some feedback. Let other people have a look over your work. Check your annual writing plan and see who you have targeted for feedback.

CONCLUSION

In this chapter you met Rowena, who used her annual writing plan to change her success rate. You now know you have to create a personalised annual writing plan. You know your most effective time to put pen to paper, and you have allocated this time in your calendar each day to write. You met Janice and Chaturanga, the grant writers who learned and worked the recipe for a successful grant. You know you have to follow the recipe, and how to expand your dot points. And you know the value of writing clearly using consistent terms and talking about the benefits of your research. So stop winging it with your writing deadlines. Start putting your annual writing plan into action and get this first draft to your first reviewer for that valuable and insightful feedback.

Now you know you can make time to write efficiently and success-fully. Your annual writing plan will guide your commitments. There is a recipe for everything you write and you have the key recipe in your kit for when you put pen to paper for your first draft. Your first draft is not your last.

In the next chapter, I will show you how feedback from the right people will have your writing singing.

CHAPTER 7 ACTIVITIES

Here are the six steps of creating an annual writing plan:

1. Take time to list all your writing commitments for the year, including speeches, articles, media publications and LinkedIn.

2. Identify the journals where your research should be submitted. Consider if you have a good cross-section of journals. Is the list extensive or too narrow? Will you have as many people as possible read your research? Have you considered the special editions for this year? Transdisciplinary research warrants your careful attention.

3. Use your annual writing plan to make writing decisions. Is the plan realistic? Or do you need to cull? Will it guide you to say no when someone asks you to do more writing this year?

4. Create a list of reviewers, those who need to know about you and your research. Allocating people and having a timeframe for when you get feedback will ensure you are not rushing.

5. Use the dates in the plan to ensure you stay on track and meet your deadlines and you are not rushing.

6. You can now craft your purpose statements for each of your writing commitments. They may change, but you will make sure that every publication sells a different aspect of your research, and that you extend your research and your researcher identity as widely as possible.

Now schedule in your personal daily writing time. Think too about where you will write. Make it safe, conducive to writing and comfortable.

On the next page is the writing plan I use myself, and with my clients. You can download this from klgcommunications.com.au.

Annual Writing Plan
Publication and Presentation Details

Items/tasks	Journal name Due date for submission	Date for review	Reviewer name	Date for review comments	Date to incorporate feedback and action

Source: Write Persuasively Toolkit, klgcommunications.com.au

*

Let's unpack the recipe for an abstract. Have a look at your latest abstract and see how closely it follows the recipe. Does it start with the **background** to your research problem, where you establish the criticality of your research? Have you followed this background detail with your **research problem**? When you have a problem, you **aim** to solve it, so have you written your aim next?

Objectives are how you achieve your aims. You only have three to five. Whether you include your objectives depends on how long your abstract is. Your readers want to know your particular **method** for solving your problem. They expect to read about your **results** or the **outcome** of your research. Ultimately, they want to know the **significance** of your research, of solving a problem of the planet, of the new knowledge you have created or what it means to your research fields. Can you recite this recipe in your sleep or tell a new researcher to your team the logical flow of this structure – the recipe for an abstract?

*

Activity 1

This is the 'magic table' I referred to in chapter 1. Now it's your turn to write persuasively by aligning your research question with your aim, objectives, outcomes and the significance of these outcomes.

Aligning your – research question + aim + objectives
+ outcome + significance

Research question	Aim	Objectives	Outcome/ deliverable	Significance
RQ 1	This research aims to 1. develop ...	This research will be achieved by (doing what?) i. identifying ...	1i	1i
		ii. evaluating ...	1ii	1ii
		iii. developing ...	1iii	1iii

Source: Write Persuasively Toolkit, klgcommunications.com.au

You can download this from klgcommunications.com.au.

Activity 2

Start talking about what your research *does* – the benefits of it – rather than describing the details of what you *do* by completing these sentences.

- This project will significantly impact ...
- This groundbreaking work ...
- This project will create local, national and international impact through ...
- This discovery of creating ... has ...
- The benefit of my research leads to ...

Keep your responses and file them in a folder called 'Why my research matters'.

*

Try this four-step process:

1. Put your purpose statement in the header of your Word document. It will then be on every page and remind you that every time you write a word and expand a dot point, it needs to add weight to your argument.

2. Leave in all your headings and subheadings. They will guide you in expanding your dot points into full sentences.

3. Define and explain the points you have made. Give evidence and examples to support your argument.

4. Be sure to write in sections, one at a time, just like the example of the scientists in the Centre for Agriculture. Stick to the process – it works. Your ideas and facts are important. Get them written down in this first draft.

You may feel uncomfortable about your ideas sounding too simple or unsophisticated because you are turning dot points into sentences, or the flow is not right. Before you go about polishing this draft, you would benefit from some feedback. Let other people have a look over your work. Check your annual writing plan and see who you have targeted for feedback.

CHAPTER 8

Step 5: Make time to revise frequently

THE SECRET TO GOOD WRITING

The secret to good writing is constant revision. Revising makes your documents great, easy to read and successful. Revising has two components:

- getting feedback
- editing.

To succeed as a researcher, you have to make progress with your writing, which means you need to be brave and seek feedback.

Feedback is not just to critique your writing – it can identify your strengths and validate your ideas. Then you can edit your work to improve the overall quality of your document. This means checking the grammar, punctuation, spelling and syntax are correct. The time you put into revising, getting feedback and editing your first draft will turn your document into a better second and third draft. With this process, you will have a successful document.

It's not easy to put your writing out there in the world for others to critique, but feedback improves your work and builds your confidence as a writer. When you get feedback from the right people, it will improve your chances of being published and accepted by your readers. Feedback can be one on one or in a group. A writing circle is a useful form of group feedback, where you receive feedback from a range of perspectives, from people who are impartial and not emotionally involved in your writing. I'll explain later in this chapter how everyone can benefit from a writing circle.

The ultimate strategy for revising is to get feedback during the process of writing your document on the writing in progress. I'm not talking about getting your final document edited in a rush a day or two before you have to submit it. This is not feedback. It's hard for people to give you considered input when you rush them. They end up giving you a quick edit in the time available, and it won't improve your writing much.

Most of us have had awful experiences with feedback, so you might be reluctant to ask. Maybe it wasn't constructive, or it was petty, or it was only an edit and just about the grammar. Perhaps you have taken feedback personally when it was really just about your writing.

In this chapter we're going to look at how to make receiving feedback a joy. This will help you to be brave and seek feedback. Plan who gives you feedback on your writing. Plan ahead for when you would benefit from feedback so it is constructive, will be effective and is something you will look forward to. Make time to revise based on your feedback. You don't have to use all the input you receive but do think about why your reviewer said what they did.

Your writing has a greater chance of success – getting you and your ideas published, or funding coming your way – if you give careful thought to the feedback you receive. Your writing can promote you sooner because you will stand out.

> Katherine chose a mentor to work with and to provide feedback on her writing. She explained her interactions with her writing mentor as:
>
> ' ... *being in a room filled with questions and ideas. Often she drew ideas out of me I did not realise were there. We often recorded our conversations so I could put key phrases teased out of me during conversations into my writing ... It was a safe and enjoyable place to talk about research. And indeed, words on the page flowed from those meetings.*'

Think about the people you can work with, or a mentor who will give you constructive feedback about your writing. Remember, great writing comes from great revising. You need great feedback plus editing.

In this chapter, we're going to change the way you think about revising by discussing how to get feedback – identifying who can give you meaningful feedback and when, and whether they are individuals or groups. You need to establish who needs to know about your research. Cross-check your annual writing plan in chapter 7 for who needs to know who you are and what you are writing about.

To give you meaningful feedback, your reviewer needs notice. You then need to inform your reviewer of the type of feedback you want, and the components and the sections you want feedback on.

We're also going to consider a key strategy for obtaining feedback and improving your writing; that is, joining or starting a writing circle. We'll establish how amazing these can be to build confidence and skills in writing. We'll then examine what it means to edit your document. And the ultimate strategy? Knowing what it means to get feedback throughout the entire writing process – and I'll explain why you should.

CHANGING THE WAY YOU THINK ABOUT FEEDBACK

Revising starts with feedback, then editing. Know the difference. You can pay for feedback and editing or trade it as a favour. Determining writing quality is difficult, and it's your attitude to writing and the writing process that will enable you to be a more confident and independent writer who is more willing to experiment with your writing in order to have that edge. You might think you have the edge, but you cannot tell until you test it.

Incorporating feedback to refine your writing means you can take your readers on a journey through your world of extraordinary ideas rather than simply a collection of facts. You can use the best examples, create momentum and inspire your readers to take action. You can focus on the significance of your research and the problems you are solving. Carefully identify people who can move you up the mountain. Look beyond your research group. Further afield might get you closer to being the best in your field.

Refer to your work in chapter 7, where you identified experts you want to work with or people who would challenge you and stretch your brain where you know it has to go. Identify the people who can give you meaningful feedback. You want to work with these people and develop a writing relationship where you feel comfortable and challenged receiving constructive feedback.

Managing your reviewer-feedback process

Learning always takes you out of your comfort zone. That's the nature of it. So let's talk about managing your reviewer-feedback process.

You've already asked your reviewer, you've agreed on the time they will work on your writing and it is in their calendar. You can manage the type of feedback you need and the sections you want feedback on – and those you don't – and ask your reviewer to focus on those. When you ask for feedback on a maximum of five pages of your writing, your expert reviewer has a manageable amount to review. Establishing how your reviewer will provide their thoughts is part of having a constructive writing relationship.

> Take, for example, the large renewable energy company I'm working with – coaching a team of eight experts to write a winning proposal. Early in our journey, we had a workshop on how I provide feedback. I showed how I ask the writer questions and make suggestions on refining or expanding ideas using track changes, and what my shorthand and note-taking symbols mean. We discussed if this process worked for everyone, if this feedback would be useful enough for them to go about revising, if the feedback was constructive and positive, or if I, as their reviewer, needed to adjust. One noteworthy comment from the group was, 'Thank goodness your feedback says more than "So what?"' This process was important for both sides to create a constructive writing relationship. We will be working together for many pages.

You don't have to feel exposed having people read your material. This is you taking responsibility for one of the key outcomes of your work as a researcher – your writing – and finding the right people to support you and give you constructive feedback so you can revise, craft and produce writing you are proud of and that will influence.

When you find the right people to give you feedback, you will grow. It will change the way you feel about feedback and revising your documents, moving you to where you want and need to be.

> People can pay for feedback – this is one of my jobs as a writing coach. One of my clients, Cheryl, has been onwards and upwards, expanding her capacity as a researcher and leader in the sustainable development and disaster-management field. She has grown into a great writer and communicator. Cheryl wrote in an email to me, 'It has been energising and motivating to be coached in the writing and reviewing process over the last decade, propelling our research team into game-changing adventures'. Feedback builds 'communication muscles' that are essential for translating great research into meaningful action.

You might think it's too hard to find the right person, or you're too scared to ask someone, or you haven't yet enjoyed the process of receiving constructive feedback. If the first reviewer you work with isn't right, try another. Feedback can be validating, encouraging you to continue to evolve with your writing. It can build your confidence. It's far easier to get feedback and revise your ideas and arguments before you submit, as opposed to receiving the often dismissive, brief, uninformative or soul-destroying feedback from journal editors, no feedback on your grant proposal or 'apply next year' with your promotion application.

You don't have to do it all on your own. Getting to the top of the mountain means two things: being brave, and getting feedback from the people you admire and wish to work alongside. Think about who these people could be. Then identify what type of feedback you think they could offer you that would enhance the quality of your thinking, ideas, research and writing.

Who can give you feedback?		What type of feedback would you like them to offer?
People you admire	*Name of world expert goes here*	E.g. does my content align with my purpose statement?
Experts you would like to work alongside	*Name of world expert goes here*	E.g. is my work appropriate for my target readers?
Mentor	*Name of world expert goes here*	E.g. does my argument align with my vision?
People beyond your research group	*Name of world expert goes here*	E.g. does this research present the practical strategies you need?

You might think you're too early in your career to be worrying about being at the top, or it's too hard on your own, or be wondering, *won't they feel annoyed at being bothered?* But what's the worst that can happen?

If you're really having trouble gaining input from others on your work, try working in a group – try writing circles.

NO NEED TO GO IT ALONE; JOIN (OR START) A WRITING CIRCLE

My work with Brad, Scott and Hannah of a Brisbane-based ecological and environmental management consultancy has been to help their team of dedicated technical experts hone their writing skills. One of the key strategies the consultancy implemented is the use of peer-to-peer forums to provide feedback on written documents. With my academic clients, I refer to this as a 'writing circle', but this company decided to refer to their sessions as 'writer chats'. They have adapted the feedback process to make it work for them, and described it in a way that makes everyone feel comfortable about participating.

My dream is for everyone to talk about writing in the same manner they discuss the technical side of their work. If you have a technical issue, your first port of call is to talk with your colleagues. If you have a question about your writing, you can go to the same colleagues to talk about writing. This can spark engagement and conversation and a sense of community around writing.

You can build your confidence as a writer with the feedback you receive. Talking about writing in groups can be organised like the writing circle, or writer chats. Writing circles expose you to different perspectives, suggestions and questions that can improve the quality of your work and writing. They are opportunities to provide feedback on drafts of writing in progress. They aim to accelerate your individual writing skills, build writing capacity and build knowledge of the building blocks of good writing. Writing circles build a culture of sustainable writing and a community of practice. In essence, writing circles are a peer review practice, like when you submit your article to a journal. In this case, you get fabulous feedback before you submit.

Research is lonely and isolating. A writing circle allows researchers to seek feedback from others on short or small amounts of writing regularly, develop writing skills, and learn to engage in rigorous debates about good writing. The writing circle process I'm talking about means finding a time and space that can be used regularly. Writing circles function best when they are located in the same place and held at the same time. The longest-running writing circle I worked with went for eight years. Researchers knew it was there and could come along at any time during their research journey.

Writing circles get you out of your garret and into the real world of writing as a practice. It's like being part of a research group, where the output of the whole group is greater than the sum of the parts.

> Savindi was a member of the writing circle that went for eight years – she was there for three of those years. Savindi knows having technical skills is not sufficient for a PhD, and found the writing circle critical in developing her ability to clearly communicate her research to peers, supervisors and industry partners. Now an academic and supervisor, Savindi facilitates her own writing circles.
>
> Manori, a new writer to these, claimed, 'The writing circle always helps me make my writing more concise … When reading colleagues' work, I can identify writing methods that I can apply to my work. I am learning from giving feedback on their writing.'

While the longest-running circle I worked on went for eight years, another has been successful for three years and is still going. How fabulous it is to have 15 different people give you 15 different perspectives on your writing each week. When researchers establish a culture of giving and receiving feedback through a writing circle, they quickly learn the value of peer feedback. Their efforts at writing are then much more efficient and successful.

You may think you need an expert to facilitate a writing circle. But not if you set it up the right way with my guidelines, provided below. They cover the four steps of reading the manuscript, critiquing, being critiqued, and what facilitating a writing circle means. Every person is involved in each task and the peer reviewers are guided to talk about writing, first in terms of structure, then style, and then language use.

Writing circles are opportunities to provide feedback on drafts of writing in progress. The four steps of reading the manuscript, critiquing, being critiqued and facilitating mean every person is involved in each task. Note that when writers talk about writing they refer firstly to structure, then style, and then language use.

Reading the manuscript:

- Note on the manuscript anything that strikes you. These comments will be valuable for the author (even if you do not say them).

- Note first impressions, reactions from a first reading or misunderstandings.

- Point out what impresses you – stars or comments of praise for a good phrase or passage are useful.

- Write nitpicks – anything small to help the author be consistent, such as use of words, length of sentences, the flow of ideas, consistency in punctuation, grammar corrections, small queries.

- Return your comments to the author after the session. Remember to sign your name as the reader.

- Make notes to share in the critiquing sessions. Focus only on the larger issues the author asked you to address, not the nitpicks.

Critiquing:

- Each critique should be brief.
- Each critique should be strictly in turn, without interruption from anyone else.
- Each critique should be centred on some important aspect of the writing.
- Each critique should be impersonal – it's the writing that's under discussion, not the author.
- Speak to the author, not other people, as you discuss the piece.
- Criticism must be constructive and lead to the possibility of revisions. Your critique must be of use to the author.
- Never ask the author a question that might bring forth a long explanation or defence. You may ask the author only direct, factual, yes or no questions. This is not an opportunity for the author to defend their writing. They are here to 'hear' where their writing is not clear.
- Do tell the writer where you were confused, surprised, annoyed or delighted, which parts you liked, what worked for you and what didn't.
- Suggestions for how to fix something may be valuable, but should be offered respectfully.
- Expand the group discussion without repetition. If somebody has said what you wanted to say, then do say, 'I agree with so and so about such and such.' If you disagree with a previous speaker, do say so and explain why.

Being critiqued:

- Before and during the entire session, the author of the piece under discussion is SILENT. This is an essential element of the process.

- Offer no defence, explanations or excuses.
- If asked to answer a question, be sure the whole group is willing for you to do so, and be as brief as possible.
- While being critiqued, do make notes of what people say about your writing. Note any comment that keeps coming up with different people.
- When all the discussion of your writing is over, you may speak if you want. If you have a question about your piece that wasn't addressed, ask it now. In general, the best response to your hard-working critics is 'Thank you'.
- You need to hear what people 'got' from your writing, what they think needs work, what they misunderstood and understood, disliked and liked. That's what you are here for.

Facilitating the group:

- Each author makes sure manuscripts are available to their group. You can have 10 people in a group, each with one to two pages.
- Start with a volunteer author's piece, and go around from there to every person at the table who would like their work reviewed.
- The critiquing also goes around the circle, every person speaking about every piece. You can pass on a turn to critique by saying 'pass'.
- Reverse directions from time to time.

Source: Write Persuasively Toolkit, klgcommunications.com.au

If you cannot find a writing circle near you, start your own. Follow the guidelines and reap the rewards of having regular feedback any time you are writing.

Some writers may prefer to work alone in the privacy of their own space. Others may think their writing style, interests and goals don't align with the group, or that it could frustrate them and hinder their productivity. Getting input in an environment where a constructive writing culture is established will get you further. Consider the amount of time you spend after you have 'submitted' to address the feedback and expectations from a journal editor. Waiting to get feedback from a journal editor only makes it harder for you, and receiving the feedback while you are writing dramatically increases your chances of being published.

GETTING FEEDBACK THROUGHOUT THE WRITING PROCESS

I know we are at the fifth step, revision, but revision also takes place at every stage of the writing process. You must seek feedback when you think, read, plan and write so you can revise your work. Before you started reading this book, how prepared were you to be a writer? How much did you know about the writing process? Had you thought about developing your writing style so your audiences read and respect your writing, and it stands out from the rest? How much do you think you still have to learn about writing?

The time you spend getting feedback throughout your writing process means you can convey your purpose, passion and belief. You can be confident you can produce the best of yourself and your research, and that your work will change the world, solve the problems of the planet and have the impact you want. Taking time to get feedback and revise frequently starts at the first step of the writing process, back when you took time to think in chapter 4.

The writing process below clearly shows that each of the four steps requires you to get feedback and incorporate this feedback before you go onto the next stage.

The Five-Step Writing Framework

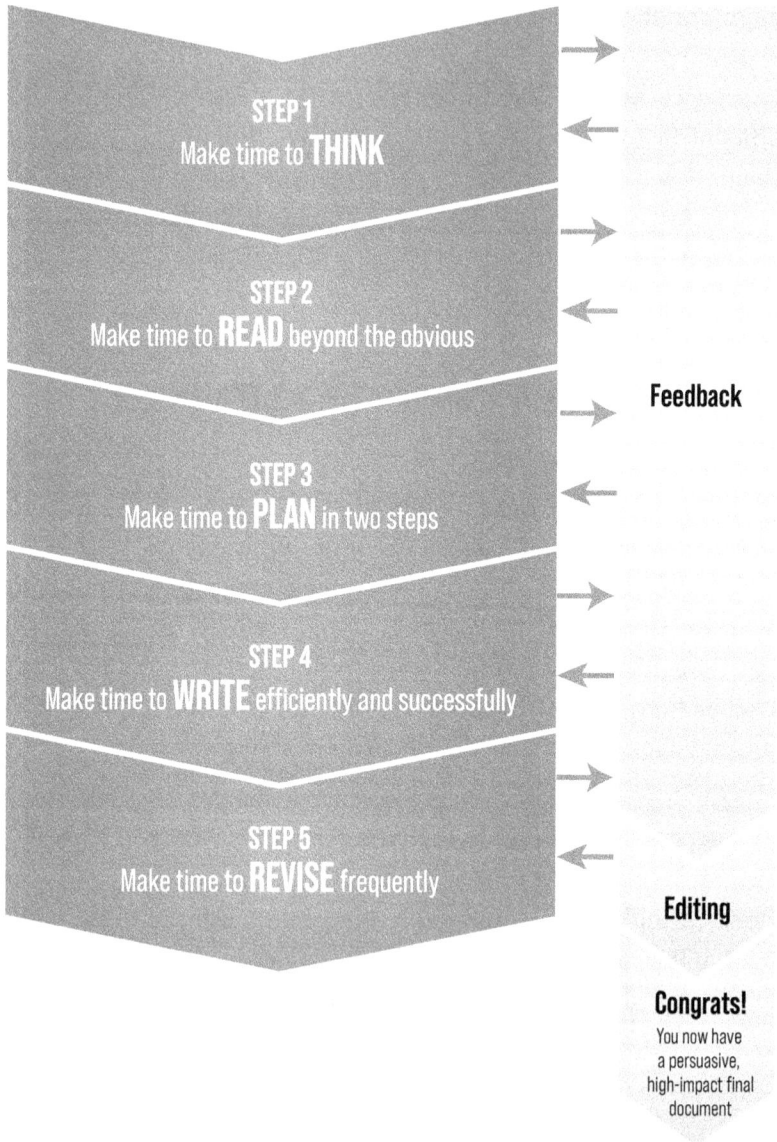

STEP 1
Make time to **THINK**

STEP 2
Make time to **READ** beyond the obvious

Feedback

STEP 3
Make time to **PLAN** in two steps

STEP 4
Make time to **WRITE** efficiently and successfully

STEP 5
Make time to **REVISE** frequently

Editing

Congrats!
You now have
a persuasive,
high-impact final
document

Source: Write Persuasively Toolkit, klgcommunications.com.au

And it is the next section that shows you exactly how to go about getting feedback, and the right sort of feedback, at each stage of the writing process.

Revising your thinking

Thinking was when you established your researcher identity – what makes you, your research and your expertise so different and valuable to your workplace or university? Writing your researcher identity requires more than one go. You wrote your first draft back in chapter 4. Now it's time for you to take your researcher identity draft to your reviewer for feedback using these questions as a guide.

Ask these questions of your reviewer:

- Do you understand my point of difference?
- Do you know what I do?
- Does the way I say it sparkle and sing?

Revising your reading

Reading was when you read beyond the obvious and identified your target research influencers. You wanted to impact as many people as possible since you were making discoveries that changed the world. You established who you are ultimately researching for and then who will spread your words farthest. You drafted your first target research influencer table in chapter 5. The feedback you are seeking here for your target research influencer table – your readers and end users – comes from beyond academia, your professional organisation or industry associations. Now take your target research influencer table to your reviewer for feedback using these three questions as a guide.

Ask these questions of your reviewer:

- Are my readers and end users different?
- Do my readers and end users come from beyond academia, my professional organisation or industry associations?
- Who else do I need to reach?

Revising your planning

In planning, you did the revolutionary two steps – your purpose statement and your rock solid dot-point plan. Well, it became rock solid after you revised your plan from that good amount of feedback you asked for back in chapter 6. You completed step four of your purpose statement when you asked for feedback and had that a-ha! moment where you knew you nailed your argument. Perhaps it was your colleagues' feedback on one of those many drafts that gave you the a-ha! moment. They gave you a clear sense of purpose that made your plan work, arguing why your research is so fantastic. Now take your purpose statement and dot-point plan to your reviewer for feedback, using the three questions below as a guide.

Ask these questions of your reviewer:

- How clear is my purpose statement?
- Do you know what I'm arguing?
- Are my dot points so clear you could write this article for me?

Revising your writing

In chapter 7, you wrote your annual writing plan and your first draft. Your annual writing plan always needs revising. Consider the researcher who had planned to share an article with me for feedback. This article was item one on her 2023 annual writing plan. She said she needed to revise her plan and get an expression of interest written for next week. She had been selected to apply for a grant. We all need money. She revised the plan, allocated time to write for the grant and identified who she needed as reviewers of her expression of interest document. This researcher has already been rewarded for adjusting her approach to writing and engaging in the revising stage! Success at the first milestone of grant rounds has also built her confidence as a writer.

That document you wrote in chapter 7 is only your first draft, not your final document. There are many people on your list of reviewers who will give you feedback. Now take your draft for feedback, using these questions as a guide.

Ask these questions of your reviewer:

Annual writing plan

- Is my annual writing plan doable?
- Does my annual writing plan have a balanced range of publication places?
- Does my annual writing plan have a smart list of reviewers?

First draft

- Is the structure of my first draft clear?
- Does my research question align with my aim?
- Are my three to five objectives clear actions that will achieve my aim?
- Do my outcomes align with my objectives?
- Is my argument clear and strong?

Revising frequently and finally

How much revising do you need to do at the end? Less if you sought feedback frequently all the way through the writing of your article, funding proposal or promotion document. Also less, again, than the time and effort you have to take to manage the resubmit feedback from the journal editors, or, worse still, if your writing was rejected. After you revise all the way through the writing process, you must polish your final document. You can use one of the many online editing tools or a professional editor. Their fresh eyes will make all the difference.

Revising your work is at least as important as writing it in the first place. The tweaking, revisiting and revising is what takes something that could be good and makes it good. Don't neglect it.*

WHAT IT MEANS TO EDIT

The second component of revising is editing. Editing is the last thing you do before you submit your documents. Allocating enough time to have your 5,000-word or 10,000-word article, funding proposal or promotion document edited makes sense. You do not edit as you write. Editing serves to improve the overall quality of your final document. It is the polishing process to ensure your readers move easily through your document – that your writing is organised, coherent and consistent in your use of words, length of sentences and flow of ideas. Editing can remove ambiguities or flaws that may stop the reader from understanding your argument. It can ensure grammar, punctuation, spelling and syntax errors do not distract your reader. I'm talking about a full and final edit of your finished

---

* www.nyti.ms/2RAji0L.

document at the end before you submit it. You can edit your document yourself, but only at the end.

During my workshops and particularly during my writing retreats, I often observe writers typing along when a blue or red line pops under a word they just typed. What do they do? They stop mid-thought and press the backspace to fix the so-labelled error. You wouldn't do this if you wrote with pen and paper. No blue or red lines there to pop up and distract you. You might feel you are being efficient in doing this, but you are not. Keep writing, get those ideas down on the page, be effective and leave the editing till the end.

One of the funny things about asking for feedback is that when you give other people your document, the first thing some do is nitpick. They find errors – the missed capital letter, a typo or the unnecessary space at the end of a word before the full stop. You do not want your reviewers to be nitpicking, so instruct them about the feedback you need. You're not asking others to read it to fix typos or punctuation. You want to know about the content and the writing. And that is why you do a full edit at the end – you don't want this nitpicking to happen in the document you submit.

You might think you know your work so well by now that you can edit some of your document along the way or that you can do just a quick edit and spot the errors, typos and inconsistencies. But you must allocate time to edit properly. There are many free online editing tools you can use. Choose one and trial it. You will be surprised how useful they are. You can also pay for a professional editor to work up your final document. Don't rush it a day or two before you have to submit. It's hard for editors to give you considered work when you rush them. They end up giving you that quick edit – what they can do with the time available – and it won't improve your writing much. Be sure to allocate time to edit so your document presents the best version of you and your research.

CONCLUSION

In this chapter, you have learned the secret of good writing is good revising, and that revising has two components – getting feedback and editing. Obtaining feedback at every stage of the writing process means you revise frequently, and then the last step is to edit your final document. You do not edit along the way.

It's not easy to put your writing out there in the world for others to critique. You have learned that when you are brave and get feedback – either one to one or in a writing circle – and act on that feedback, you will successfully convey your purpose, passion and research. You learned that revising will produce the best of you and your research and have the impact you want.

Stop writing without allowing time to revise. Your first draft is not your final draft. Identify who can give you meaningful feedback at each stage of your writing, and ask them to do so. Revise your work. Do a final edit. Ensure your document is polished and sells you and your research.

It's not often I quote a company tagline, but the magnificent pen company Montblanc has a rather brilliant one. As an ambitious researcher, ask yourself, 'What kind of future will you write today?'

CHAPTER 8 ACTIVITIES

Try this four-step process:

1. Put your purpose statement in the header of your Word document. It will then be on every page and remind you that every time you write a word and expand a dot point, it needs to add weight to your argument.

2. Leave in all your headings and subheadings. They will guide you in expanding your dot points into full sentences.

3. Define and explain the points you have made. Give evidence and examples to support your argument.

4. Be sure to write in sections, one at a time, just like the example of the scientists in the Centre for Agriculture. Stick to the process – it works. Your ideas and facts are important. Get them written down in this first draft.

*

Writing circles are opportunities to provide feedback on drafts of writing in progress. The four steps of reading the manuscript, critiquing, being critiqued and facilitating mean every person is involved in each task. Note that when writers talk about writing they refer firstly to structure, then style, and then language use.

Reading the manuscript:

- Note on the manuscript anything that strikes you. These comments will be valuable for the author (even if you do not say them).

- Note first impressions, reactions from a first reading or misunderstandings.

- Point out what impresses you – stars or comments of praise for a good phrase or passage are useful.
- Write nitpicks – anything small to help the author be consistent, such as use of words, length of sentences, the flow of ideas, consistency in punctuation, grammar corrections, small queries.
- Return your comments to the author after the session. Remember to sign your name as the reader.
- Make notes to share in the critiquing sessions. Focus only on the larger issues the author asked you to address, not the nitpicks.

Critiquing:
- Each critique should be brief.
- Each critique should be strictly in turn, without interruption from anyone else.
- Each critique should be centred on some important aspect of the writing.
- Each critique should be impersonal – it's the writing that's under discussion, not the author.
- Speak to the author, not other people, as you discuss the piece.
- Criticism must be constructive and lead to the possibility of revisions. Your critique must be of use to the author.
- Never ask the author a question that might bring forth a long explanation or defence. You may ask the author only direct, factual, yes or no questions. This is not an opportunity for the author to defend their writing. They are here to 'hear' where their writing is not clear.
- Do tell the writer where you were confused, surprised, annoyed or delighted, which parts you liked, what worked for you and what didn't.

- Suggestions for how to fix something may be valuable, but should be offered respectfully.
- Expand the group discussion without repetition. If somebody has said what you wanted to say, then do say, 'I agree with so and so about such and such.' If you disagree with a previous speaker, do say so and explain why.

Being critiqued:

- Before and during the entire session, the author of the piece under discussion is SILENT. This is an essential element of the process.
- Offer no defence, explanations or excuses.
- If asked to answer a question, be sure the whole group is willing for you to do so, and be as brief as possible.
- While being critiqued, do make notes of what people say about your writing. Note any comment that keeps coming up with different people.
- When all the discussion of your writing is over, you may speak if you want. If you have a question about your piece that wasn't addressed, ask it now. In general, the best response to your hard-working critics is 'Thank you'.
- You need to hear what people 'got' from your writing, what they think needs work, what they misunderstood and understood, disliked and liked. That's what you are here for.

Facilitating the group:

- Each author makes sure manuscripts are available to their group. You can have 10 people in a group, each with one to two pages.
- Start with a volunteer author's piece, and go around from there to every person at the table who would like their work reviewed.

- The critiquing also goes around the circle, every person speaking about every piece. You can pass on a turn to critique by saying 'pass'.
- Reverse directions from time to time.

Source: Write Persuasively Toolkit, klgcommunications.com.au

Conclusion

Make time for the part of your life where you write about your research. Find the time to write brilliantly in a way that changes the world.

Follow my five-step time allocation process and you will transform the way you write. Your writing will be much more impactful. Thinking, reading, planning, writing and revising creates writing that matters. You will craft words that influence and persuade.

Think of yourself as a writer, a writer of research, so when you sit down to write, you are excited rather than anxious. You willingly engage in the process of persuading your readers your research matters. This new approach to your written word will transform your funding proposals, your promotion applications and your articles. When your funding proposal is successful, you will set yourself up for the next three to five years, and launch yourself into the position of expert. When your vision for the next five years is acknowledged with a phone call, your promotion application will have been successful. When you are invited by the world expert to present as the keynote speaker, it's based on your latest publication.

This is the world where your discoveries change the world and where your research changes lives. You help children survive disease, you build water security and give people access to clean water. You save the Great Barrier Reef. This world is available to you if you put in the work I have suggested in this book.

I have shown you a five-step process to write persuasively. Along with your research, your ability to write persuasively is needed for you to succeed and flourish in your career.

Most people don't make time for their writing. In my world, writing is only one-fifth of the writing process. After your research, you need to:

1. Make time to think – smooth the way to completion.
2. Make time to read – nail who will benefit from your research.
3. Make time to plan – revolutionise your purpose and your dot-point plan.
4. Make time to write – personalise your annual writing plan and collate your recipes.
5. Make time to revise – be brave and revise frequently.

Do this and you'll be doing things few ever make time to do. Every percentage point you get above the average gives your funding proposal, your promotion application or your article a greater chance of success.

It's the time, right? You don't have it. It's probably the biggest barrier. Everyone I've worked with says they haven't got time to do even the writing part, and here I am, telling you to add another four stages. But the time you take right now will save you so much time later that this writing process will become effortless and second nature.

Imagine every researcher being able to efficiently communicate the value of what they are doing and influence decision makers. This is the world I'm trying to create. I want you to succeed. I know you are ambitious. My dream world is where everyone talks about writing, where the five stages – thinking, reading, planning, writing and revising – become effortless and second nature and everyone is crushing it.

Be ambitious. Write the change you want to see in the world. Make time to write persuasively.

I run regular workshops and writing retreats.
Go to klgcommunications.com.au for more information.

www.ingramcontent.com/pod-product-compliance
Lightning Source LLC
Chambersburg PA
CBHW060233030426
42335CB00014B/1430